PRAGUE
TRAVEL GUIDE
2025

Experience the Magic of Central Europe: Explore, Discover, and Immerse

Vale Lillian

Dear Readers,

Prague is more than a destination, it's a storybook come to life. With every cobblestone, spire, and hidden alley, the city invites you to lose yourself in its magic.

This guide is my love letter to Prague, filled with tips and stories to help you experience its charm in your own way. Let it lead you to moments that will stay in your heart forever.

Happy exploring!

Warmly,
[Vale Lillian]

TABLE OF CONTENT

- Language Tips: Essential Czech Phrases

Getting to and Around Prague

- How to Get to Prague: Flights, Trains, and Buses
- Public Transportation: Trams, Metros, and Buses
- Walking and Biking in the City
- Car Rentals and Taxis

Where to Stay in Prague

- Best Neighborhoods to Stay In
- Budget-Friendly Accommodations
- Mid-Range Hotels and Apartments
- Luxury Stays for a Lavish Experience

Exploring Prague's Must-See Attractions

- Prague Castle: A Step into Royalty

- Charles Bridge: An Icon of the City
- Old Town Square and the Astronomical Clock
- St. Vitus Cathedral: Gothic Masterpiece
- The Jewish Quarter: History and Heritage

Hidden Corners and Lesser-Known Gems

- Off-the-Beaten-Path Neighborhoods
- Secret Gardens and Quiet Spots
- Unique Museums and Galleries

A Foodie's Guide to Prague

- Traditional Czech Dishes You Must Try
- Best Restaurants and Cafés
- Vegan and Vegetarian Options
- Prague's Craft Beer Scene

Experiencing Prague by Day and Night

- Daytime Adventures: Parks, Markets, and More
- Prague After Dark: Bars, Nightclubs, and Cultural Performances

Shopping in Prague

- Souvenirs Worth Taking Home
- Local Markets and Boutiques
- High-End Shopping Streets

Day Trips and Excursions

- Český Krumlov: A Fairytale Town
- Kutná Hora and the Bone Church
- Karlovy Vary: Spa Heaven

Practical Information for Travelers

- Currency, Costs, and Tipping in Prague
- Health and Safety Tips
- Emergency Contacts and Numbers
- Accessibility and Inclusivity

Seasonal Events and Festivals

- prague Spring International Music Festival
- Christmas Markets and Winter Festivities
- Other Annual Celebrations

Sustainable Travel in Prague

- Eco-Friendly Accommodations
- Supporting Local Businesses
- Reducing Your Travel Footprint

Conclusion

Chapter one

Introduction

Welcome to Prague

Prague is the kind of city that stays with you long after you've left. Whether it's your first time here or your tenth, the magic of this place always finds a way to surprise you. It's not just the beauty of the city though Prague is breathtaking in every sense. It's also the rhythm of life here, a mix of old-world charm and modern vibrance that feels both comforting and exciting.

As I sat down to write this guide, I thought about what makes Prague so special. For me, it's the way the city feels alive with stories. Every street corner, every building, every bridge seems to carry whispers of its past. You'll see it in the Gothic towers that rise against the sky, in the baroque churches that glimmer with gold, and in the bustling markets that have stood for centuries. But Prague is more than just a place frozen in time. It's a city that embraces the now through its art, its food, its music, and the warmth of its people.

This guide is my invitation for you to see Prague through my eyes. It's not just about visiting the famous landmarks, though of course, you'll find plenty of tips on those. It's about experiencing the heartbeat of the city. It's about finding a quiet moment in a tucked-away café, hearing a street musician play something that moves you, or simply watching the world go by as you sip on a perfectly poured Czech beer.

In these pages, you'll find everything you need to plan your trip. There's practical advice like when to go, how to get around, and what to pack and plenty of suggestions for what to see, eat, and do. But beyond that, I want this book to help you connect with Prague in a deeper way. I want you to feel like you're traveling with a friend who knows the city well, someone who's eager to show you not just where to go, but how to feel at home here.

Prague has something for everyone. Maybe you're drawn to the grandeur of Prague Castle or the quiet beauty of a hidden courtyard. Perhaps you're here to explore the city's rich history, or maybe you're looking forward to indulging in its vibrant culinary scene. Whatever it is that brings you here, I promise Prague won't disappoint.

And it's not just about the big moments. Yes, standing on the Charles Bridge at sunrise is unforgettable, and seeing the Astronomical Clock chime is a must. But it's also the small, unexpected things that make Prague so enchanting. It's the sound of church bells echoing across the city, the scent of fresh trdelník wafting through the air, the way the Vltava River sparkles in the afternoon light.

This guide is designed to help you make the most of your time here, but it's also a reminder to slow down and savor the journey. Prague isn't a city to rush through. It's a place to linger, to explore, to let yourself get a little lost. Because sometimes, it's when you're not looking for anything in particular that you stumble upon something unforgettable.

As you flip through these pages, I hope you'll feel inspired to create your own story in Prague. Whether it's a story of discovery, relaxation, adventure, or all of the above, I can't wait for you to experience everything this incredible city has to offer.

So, welcome to Prague, and welcome to your adventure. Let's make it one to remember.

Why Prague Should Be on Your Travel List

Prague is a city that effortlessly bridges the past and present, offering a travel experience like no other. It's a destination where centuries-old architecture, cultural richness, and vibrant modernity coexist, making it an ideal choice for anyone seeking to immerse themselves in history, beauty, and adventure. Whether you're a seasoned traveler or someone planning your first big trip, Prague has something to captivate every type of visitor.

First, there's the undeniable allure of Prague's history. This city has witnessed everything from medieval glory to modern transformation, and it wears its history proudly. Walking through its streets is like stepping back in time, with Gothic cathedrals, baroque palaces, and Renaissance courtyards telling stories of a bygone era. Landmarks like Prague Castle, Charles Bridge, and the Astronomical Clock are more than just impressive sights they're windows into the city's soul, connecting you to the people and events that shaped its character.

But Prague isn't just about looking back. It's a thriving, dynamic city where tradition meets innovation. The creative energy here is infectious, whether you're exploring contemporary art galleries, catching a live music performance, or savoring dishes that blend Czech culinary heritage with modern twists. Prague is a place where old and new come together in perfect harmony, making it an endlessly fascinating destination.

For food lovers, Prague is nothing short of a paradise. Imagine savoring hearty Czech classics like svíčková or goulash in a cozy restaurant, paired with a glass of world-famous Czech beer. Craving something sweet? Indulge in a fresh pastry from a local bakery or try a trdelník, a warm, cinnamon-sugar-coated treat that feels like a hug in dessert form. And with an increasing number of vegetarian, vegan, and international dining options, Prague's food scene is more diverse than ever.

Then there's the city's unique vibe. Prague is vibrant yet unhurried, bustling yet peaceful. It's a place where you can enjoy the lively atmosphere of Old Town Square one moment and find yourself in a serene garden or quiet alley the next. The city encourages you to explore at your own pace, whether that means hopping on a tram to a less-visited neighborhood or simply sitting by the Vltava River and watching the world go by.

What truly sets Prague apart, though, is its accessibility. The city is incredibly walkable, with most major attractions located within a compact area. Public transportation is efficient and easy to navigate, making it simple to get around without stress. Prague is also an affordable European destination, offering incredible value for your money when it comes to accommodations, food, and activities.

Finally, Prague's charm lies in the way it resonates with every kind of traveler. Are you a history enthusiast? Prague will fascinate you. A hopeless romantic? The city's dreamy streets and illuminated bridges will steal your heart. An adventurer? Prague's eclectic neighborhoods and surrounding countryside are waiting to be explored. Or maybe you're simply looking for a place to relax and recharge Prague can do that too, with its cozy cafés, tranquil parks, and warm hospitality.

In short, Prague isn't just a destination; it's an experience. It's a city that invites you to slow down, soak in the atmosphere, and let yourself be inspired. Whether you come for a weekend or a week, it promises to leave you with memories you'll treasure for a lifetime. So if you're looking for a place that offers history, culture, beauty, and heart, Prague deserves to be at the very top of your travel list.

How to Use This Guide

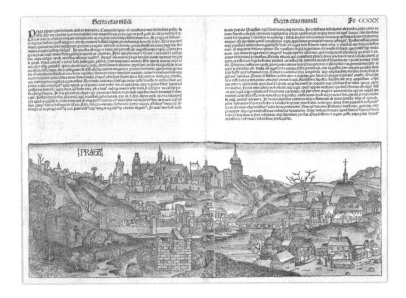

Welcome to *Prague Travel Guide 2025*! This book is designed to be your trusted companion as you navigate the enchanting streets of Prague, discover its treasures, and make the most of your visit. Whether you're planning every detail in advance or prefer to go with the flow, this guide will help you explore the city with confidence and ease.

Here's how to get the most out of it:

1. Start with the Big Picture

The introduction offers a foundation for understanding what makes Prague so special. By reading the sections "Welcome to Prague" and "Why Prague Should Be on Your Travel List," you'll gain insights into the city's character, history, and unique appeal. These chapters set the tone for your adventure, inspiring you to dive deeper into everything Prague has to offer.

2. Plan Your Trip with Practical Advice

In the "Planning Your Trip to Prague" chapter, you'll find essential information to make your travel experience smooth and stress-free. From choosing the best time to visit to tips on packing, budgeting, and understanding local customs, this section equips you with all the practical knowledge you need before you even step foot in the city.

3. Explore at Your Own Pace

The guide is organized to cater to different types of travelers. Whether you're looking for iconic landmarks, quiet corners, or local experiences, you'll find detailed chapters dedicated to sightseeing, dining, shopping, and nightlife. Each section is designed to provide a mix of must-see highlights and recommendations that let you experience Prague your way.

4. Use the Neighborhood Breakdown

Prague is a city of distinct neighborhoods, each with its own personality and charm. This guide divides the city into key districts, making it easier for you to explore one area at a time. Use these chapters to learn what makes each neighborhood special, including tips on how to get there, where to eat, and what to do.

5. Follow Suggested Themes and Interests

Whether you're a history buff, an art lover, a foodie, or someone who loves a bit of everything, this guide offers tailored suggestions to match your interests. Look for sections that highlight specific themes, like Prague's historical landmarks, its culinary scene, or its vibrant arts and culture.

6. Stay Flexible and Spontaneous

While the guide provides a wealth of information, it's also meant to encourage flexibility. If something unexpected catches your eye—a street musician playing a tune you can't resist, a café that feels too inviting to pass up, or an unplanned walk along the Vltava—follow your instincts. Some of the best travel memories come from moments you don't plan.

7. Make the Most of Practical Information

In addition to recommendations, this guide is packed with practical tips. Look for advice on using public transportation, finding the best local spots, and staying safe during your trip. The "Practical Information" chapter at the end of the book serves as a quick reference for any questions that come up during your journey.

8. Use the Map and Resources

For easy navigation, this guide includes maps to help you locate key attractions, dining spots, and transit options. Additionally, the appendices feature a Czech phrasebook, helpful websites, and reading recommendations for those who want to delve deeper into Prague's history and culture.

9. Think Beyond the City

Prague is incredible, but the Czech Republic has so much more to offer. The "Day Trips and Excursions" chapter highlights nearby destinations that are perfect for short trips, whether you're interested in castles, charming towns, or scenic escapes.

10. Let It Be Your Companion

This guide is meant to be more than just a book—it's your travel partner. You'll find personal insights, stories, and suggestions woven throughout the pages, designed to help you feel connected to the city as you explore.

As you use this guide, remember that it's here to make your trip enjoyable and memorable. Whether you're planning everything in advance or flipping through its pages while wandering Prague's streets, it's a resource you can rely on to answer questions, spark ideas, and guide your adventure.

Enjoy the journey, and let Prague surprise and delight you at every turn. Happy travels!

Chapter Two

A Glimpse into Prague's History and Culture

From Medieval Times to the Modern Era

Prague's history is like a living storybook, where each chapter has left its mark on the city's streets, buildings, and spirit. It's a tale of resilience, transformation, and a deep cultural legacy that continues to shape the Prague you see today. To truly understand this city, it helps to look back at how it has evolved from its medieval beginnings to the thriving modern metropolis it is now.

The Foundations of a Medieval City

Prague's story begins in the 9th century when the Přemyslid dynasty established a settlement on the banks of the Vltava River. By the 10th century, Prague had grown into a bustling trading hub, connecting Western and Eastern Europe. The construction of Prague Castle, started in 870, was a pivotal moment, marking the city's rise as a political and cultural center.

The medieval period saw Prague flourish under the reign of Charles IV in the 14th century. As King of Bohemia and Holy Roman Emperor, Charles IV transformed the city into a European capital. He

23

founded Charles University in 1348—the first university in Central Europe—and commissioned many of Prague's iconic landmarks, including Charles Bridge and St. Vitus Cathedral. His vision turned Prague into a beacon of education, architecture, and art, earning it the nickname "The Golden City."

Renaissance and Baroque Splendor

The Renaissance brought a new wave of creativity to Prague, visible in the city's elegant palaces and courtyards. The court of Emperor Rudolf II in the late 16th century became a hub for scientists, artists, and thinkers, including the astronomers Tycho Brahe and Johannes Kepler. Rudolf's fascination with alchemy and the occult gave Prague an air of mystery that still lingers in its narrow streets and hidden gardens.

The 17th and 18th centuries were marked by the grandeur of the Baroque era. This period left Prague with opulent churches, grand squares, and elaborate statues that continue to define the city's skyline. The Old Town and Lesser Town were filled with architectural masterpieces like the Church of St. Nicholas, showcasing Prague's status as a cultural jewel of Europe.

A City of Revolution and Change

The 19th century was a time of great change for Prague as it became a center of the Czech National Revival. This movement aimed to preserve Czech language, culture, and identity during a period of growing nationalism under the Austro-Hungarian Empire. Writers, poets, and composers like Bedřich Smetana and Antonín Dvořák used their work to express pride in Czech heritage, solidifying Prague's role as a cultural hub.

The early 20th century brought further upheaval. After World War I, Prague became the capital of the newly formed Czechoslovakia, a moment of great pride for its citizens. However, this independence was short-lived. During World War II, Nazi Germany occupied the city, and Prague's Jewish community faced devastating losses.

After the war, Czechoslovakia fell under Soviet influence, ushering in decades of communist rule. The Prague Spring of 1968 was a bold attempt at political reform, but it was brutally suppressed by the Soviet military. Despite this, Prague's spirit remained unbroken, and in 1989, the Velvet Revolution peacefully ended communist rule, leading to the formation of the Czech Republic in 1993.

Prague in the Modern Era

Today, Prague stands as a testament to its rich and complex history. It's a city that has embraced modernity without losing its connection to the past. The medieval heart of the city remains intact, with its cobblestone streets, ancient bridges, and historic squares offering glimpses into earlier times. Meanwhile, contemporary Prague buzzes with life, filled with innovative art, cutting-edge technology, and a thriving local culture.

Prague's journey from its medieval origins to the modern era is a story of survival, creativity, and reinvention. It's a city that honors its past while looking toward the future, making it a truly unique destination for anyone who visits.

Key Historical Events That Shaped Prague

Prague's identity as one of Europe's most remarkable cities has been molded by centuries of pivotal events. These moments, both triumphant and tumultuous, have left an indelible mark on the city, shaping its character and resilience. To understand Prague today, it's essential to explore the defining events that have written its story.

The Reign of Charles IV (1346–1378)

The 14th century was a golden age for Prague, thanks to the visionary leadership of Charles IV, King of Bohemia and Holy Roman Emperor. During his reign, Prague became the capital of the Holy Roman Empire and a center of culture, education, and architecture. Charles founded Charles University in 1348, making it the oldest university in Central Europe, and he oversaw the construction of iconic landmarks like Charles Bridge and St. Vitus Cathedral. His reign elevated Prague to prominence and laid the foundation for its enduring legacy as a European cultural hub.

The Defenestration of Prague (1618)

Few events encapsulate Prague's fiery spirit like the Defenestration of Prague, which took place in 1618. This dramatic act involved the throwing of two imperial officials out of a castle window by Protestant nobles, sparking the Thirty Years' War—a conflict that ravaged much of Europe. The event symbolized Prague's central role in the struggle for religious and political freedom, a theme that resonates throughout its history.

The Habsburg Rule and Czech National Revival (1620–1918)

The defeat of Bohemian forces at the Battle of White Mountain in 1620 marked the beginning of Habsburg domination, a period that saw the suppression of Czech culture and language. Yet, even under foreign rule, Prague's identity persisted. By the 19th century, the Czech National Revival movement emerged, championing the preservation of Czech heritage. Writers, composers, and intellectuals like František Palacký and Bedřich Smetana used their work to reignite national pride, setting the stage for Prague's resurgence as a cultural capital.

World War II and the Holocaust (1939–1945)

World War II was a dark chapter in Prague's history. Under Nazi occupation, the city suffered tremendous losses, particularly within its Jewish community. Once a vibrant part of Prague's fabric, the Jewish population was decimated by the Holocaust. Despite this tragedy, Prague's Old Jewish Cemetery and synagogues stand today as powerful reminders of the city's enduring spirit and its commitment to preserving its history.

The Prague Spring and Soviet Occupation (1968)

In 1968, Prague became the epicenter of a bold attempt at reform known as the Prague Spring. Led by Alexander Dubček, this movement aimed to create "socialism with a human face" by introducing political and economic freedoms. However, the Soviet Union viewed these reforms as a threat, and Warsaw Pact troops invaded Prague to crush the uprising. The event left an indelible scar on the city, but it also galvanized its people's determination for change.

The Velvet Revolution (1989)

One of Prague's most defining moments came in 1989 with the Velvet Revolution, a peaceful movement that ended decades of communist rule in Czechoslovakia. Citizens gathered in Wenceslas Square, their voices united in the call for freedom and democracy. The revolution's success not only transformed the nation but also symbolized Prague's enduring role as a beacon of resilience and hope.

The Formation of the Czech Republic (1993)

After the peaceful dissolution of Czechoslovakia in 1993, Prague became the capital of the newly formed Czech Republic. This moment marked a new chapter for the city, one of independence and growth. Since then, Prague has embraced its role as a global destination while maintaining its unique blend of history and modernity.

Prague in the 21st Century

Today, Prague stands as a city shaped by its past but not defined by it. It has emerged from centuries of conflict and change as a vibrant, dynamic metropolis. Its preserved medieval core, cultural landmarks, and innovative spirit continue to draw visitors from around the world. Prague's story is one of resilience, creativity, and an unwavering commitment to its identity.

By understanding these key historical events, you'll gain a deeper appreciation for Prague's incredible journey. Each moment has contributed to the city's character, making it the extraordinary destination it is today.

Prague's Rich Cultural Tapestry: Art, Music, and Literature

Prague is a city where creativity thrives, and its artistic and cultural legacy is woven into every corner of the city. From classical music to modern art, from world-renowned literature to innovative theater, Prague has long been a beacon of artistic expression and intellectual achievement. The city's rich cultural tapestry is a testament to its enduring passion for creativity, and its influence can be seen and felt in nearly every aspect of Prague's daily life.

A Legacy of Music

Prague's connection to music is legendary, and it has earned a place among Europe's most important musical cities. The works of composers like Antonín Dvořák, Bedřich Smetana, and Leoš Janáček echo through the city's concert halls and theaters. The famous *Vltava* (also known as *The Moldau*) by Smetana, a symphonic poem that captures the spirit of the Czech countryside, is just one example of how Prague's composers have expressed national pride through music.

The city's love for classical music is palpable in its world-class venues, such as the State Opera, the Rudolfinum, and the Municipal House. These historic buildings continue to host performances by leading orchestras and conductors from around the world. Prague is also home to the Prague Spring International Music Festival, one of the most prestigious classical music festivals in Europe. Whether you're enjoying a performance of Dvořák's *New World Symphony* or hearing a contemporary composition, Prague's musical heritage is alive and well, offering something for every type of music lover.

The Art Scene: From the Old Masters to Contemporary Innovation

Prague's art scene is as diverse as it is vibrant. The city's galleries and museums hold masterpieces from the Old Masters, including works by renowned artists like Peter Paul Rubens, Caravaggio, and Rembrandt. The National Gallery, with its impressive collection of European art, is a must-see for any art lover. But Prague's artistic soul is not confined to the classical. The city has long been a hub for modern and contemporary art, from the revolutionary work of Czech artists like Toyen and František Kupka to today's cutting-edge installations and exhibits.

Prague's eclectic mix of galleries, street art, and public sculptures ensures that art is never far from sight.

Walking through the city, you'll encounter sculptures by David Černý, whose thought-provoking, sometimes controversial works challenge perceptions and provoke conversation. One such piece, the famous *Kaufmann House* with its twisting figure, embodies the playful yet profound nature of Prague's modern art scene.

Literature: A City of Writers and Poets

Prague has been the home and inspiration for some of the most influential writers and poets in the world. Perhaps the most famous is Franz Kafka, whose works, such as *The Trial* and *Metamorphosis*, are steeped in themes of existentialism, isolation, and absurdity. Kafka's presence is still felt throughout

Prague, and his former home and the Kafka Museum offer a glimpse into the mind of one of the 20th century's most enigmatic literary figures.

In addition to Kafka, Prague has been the birthplace of many other influential writers, including Milan Kundera, whose *The Unbearable Lightness of Being* explores the complexities of life in Soviet-occupied Czechoslovakia, and poet Jaroslav Seifert, a Nobel Prize winner whose work captured the spirit of Prague's people. The city is filled with literary landmarks, from cozy cafés where writers once gathered to bookshops that offer both Czech and international works. Prague's literary heritage continues to inspire contemporary authors and poets, making it a city that still lives and breathes through words.

The Theater: A Rich Tradition of Performance

Prague has also earned a reputation for its thriving theater scene, which blends traditional performances with innovative, avant-garde productions. The National Theatre and the Estates Theatre are among the city's most important cultural institutions, hosting both Czech classics and international plays. The Estates Theatre is particularly notable as the venue where Mozart's *Don Giovanni* was first performed in 1787, adding another layer of history to its already significant role in the city's cultural life.

The Czech tradition of puppet theater, which dates back to the 18th century, continues to captivate audiences in Prague. The Prague Marionette Theatre and other venues showcase this unique form of artistic expression, blending humor, drama, and artistry in ways that are uniquely Czech.

A City Where Culture Lives and Breathes

Prague's artistic and cultural heritage is not just a relic of the past—it is alive and thriving in the city's streets, its festivals, its museums, and its people. The city offers something for every creative soul, whether it's the opportunity to experience world-class music, explore centuries-old art, read timeless literature, or enjoy an unforgettable theater performance.

As you wander through Prague, take a moment to appreciate how art, music, and literature intertwine, giving the city its unique atmosphere. Whether you are a lover of the classical or a seeker of the contemporary, Prague's rich cultural tapestry ensures that every visit is a journey through the creative heart of Europe.

Chapter Three

Planning Your Trip to Prague

Best Times to Visit

Prague is a city that welcomes visitors all year round, but the timing of your trip can significantly impact the experience you'll have. Whether you're hoping to enjoy Prague's outdoor charm, explore its historic sites with fewer crowds, or immerse yourself in its vibrant cultural scene, understanding the best times to visit can help you tailor your trip to fit your preferences. Let's explore what each season in Prague has to offer and help you decide when is the perfect time for your adventure.

Spring: The City Awakens (March to May)

Spring is one of the most magical times to visit Prague. The city shakes off the chill of winter and begins to bloom with life. Temperatures start to rise, typically ranging from 10°C (50°F) in March to around 20°C (68°F) by May. The mild weather makes it a perfect time for sightseeing, and the city's parks and gardens come alive with colorful flowers.

One of the highlights of spring in Prague is the Easter season, which brings a host of cultural and religious events. The Easter markets in Old Town Square and Wenceslas Square are a delightful sight, offering handmade crafts, delicious local food, and traditional Easter eggs. With fewer tourists than in the summer months, spring offers a more peaceful experience, allowing you to enjoy the city at a more relaxed pace.

Summer: Bustling and Lively (June to August)

Summer in Prague is vibrant and full of energy, as the city attracts tourists from all over the world. The weather is warm, with temperatures ranging from 20°C (68°F) to 30°C (86°F), perfect for enjoying outdoor activities. It's a great time for leisurely strolls along the Vltava River, sitting at outdoor cafés, or visiting Prague's many parks and gardens.

Summer also brings a packed calendar of events and festivals. The Prague Summer Festival, with its mix of classical music, opera, and theater performances, draws large crowds to the city's historic venues. The city is at its most lively, with street performers, food stalls, and open-air events filling the streets. However, this is also the peak tourist season, so expect larger crowds, especially around the major attractions like Prague Castle, Charles Bridge, and Old Town Square. If you prefer a more tranquil experience, it might be wise to visit in the early part of the season before the crowds reach their peak in July and August.

Autumn: Crisp Air and Fall Colors (September to November)

Autumn is another excellent time to visit Prague. The weather remains mild in September and October, with temperatures averaging between 15°C (59°F) and 25°C (77°F), making it a comfortable time for sightseeing. The city's parks and gardens turn into a stunning display of fall colors, creating a picturesque backdrop for your adventures.

September marks the end of the busy tourist season, so while the city still retains some energy, it's much quieter compared to the summer months. By November, the city begins to slow down, offering a more peaceful experience, particularly in the historic parts of the city. This is also the time when the Christmas markets start to set up, especially the iconic ones in Old Town and Wenceslas Square. The crisp autumn air, combined with the early holiday season buzz, makes Prague a charming place to visit during this time.

Winter: A Fairytale Wonderland (December to February)

Winter in Prague has its own kind of magic. While temperatures can drop to around -5°C (23°F) or lower, the city transforms into a winter wonderland, especially if you're lucky enough to experience a light dusting of snow. Winter offers a more intimate and romantic atmosphere, with fewer tourists and the chance to enjoy the city's beauty without the crowds.

One of the most enchanting aspects of winter in Prague is the Christmas season. The Christmas markets that open in late November and run through December are an absolute highlight. Stalls overflowing with handcrafted goods, mulled wine, and traditional Czech treats fill the squares, and the festive lights make the city look like a scene from a fairytale. If you enjoy winter sports, Prague's ice rinks provide an opportunity to glide on the ice while surrounded by the stunning medieval architecture.

Although the cold can be a factor, the winter season offers a quieter, more reflective experience. It's a great time to visit Prague's cozy cafés, enjoy hearty Czech cuisine, and explore the city's historical sites without the usual summer rush.

Choosing Your Ideal Time

Each season in Prague offers something special, and the best time to visit really depends on what kind of experience you're looking for. If you love festivals, vibrant street life, and warm weather, summer might be the right time for you. If you prefer fewer crowds and enjoy the beauty of the changing seasons, spring and autumn offer a perfect balance. Winter, with its fairytale charm, is ideal if you want a more intimate experience of Prague, with the added bonus of Christmas markets and cozy atmospheres.

No matter when you visit, Prague will leave you with lasting memories of its historic charm, cultural richness, and unique beauty.

Essential Travel Documents

When planning your trip to Prague, it's crucial to ensure you have the right travel documents in order to make your journey as smooth and hassle-free as possible. While the process of organizing your paperwork may seem daunting, with a little preparation, you can avoid any last-minute stress. Here's a detailed guide to the essential travel documents you'll need before heading to Prague, whether you're visiting from another European Union country or traveling from farther abroad.

Passport

Your passport is your most important travel document when visiting Prague, especially if you're coming from outside the Schengen Area. Make sure your passport is valid for at least six months beyond your planned departure date from the Czech Republic. This is a standard requirement for most countries, as it ensures that you're not entering with an expiring passport. If you need to renew it before your trip, give yourself plenty of time to process the renewal.

If you're traveling from a European Union country or another country within the Schengen Area, you may not need a passport at all. Instead, a valid national ID card is usually sufficient for entry. However, it's always a good idea to check the specific entry requirements for your nationality prior to travel, as rules can occasionally change.

Visa Requirements

Whether or not you need a visa to visit Prague depends on your nationality. The Czech Republic is part of the Schengen Area, so citizens of many countries, including the United States, Canada,

Australia, and most EU member states, do not need a visa for stays of up to 90 days.

If you're planning to stay longer than 90 days, you'll need to apply for a long-term visa or residency permit, depending on the purpose of your stay. If you're from a country that requires a visa to enter the Schengen Area, you'll need to apply for a short-stay Schengen visa, which is valid for travel within all Schengen member states.

To apply for a visa, you'll typically need to provide documents such as your passport, proof of accommodation, travel insurance, financial proof of funds, and possibly a flight itinerary. Be sure to check with the Czech embassy or consulate in your country for specific visa application requirements and processing times, as these can vary.

Travel Insurance

While not a requirement for entry, travel insurance is highly recommended when traveling to Prague. It provides coverage in case of unexpected events such as medical emergencies, lost luggage, or flight cancellations. Travel insurance is especially important if you're traveling from outside the EU, as healthcare services in the Czech Republic may not be covered by your home country's insurance.

You should consider purchasing a travel insurance policy that includes medical coverage, emergency evacuation, and coverage for trip interruptions or cancellations. It's also worth noting that if you plan to drive in Prague or any other part of the Czech Republic, you'll need to have appropriate car rental insurance as part of your travel policy.

Flight and Accommodation Confirmation

While not required for entry, it's wise to have a copy of your flight reservation and accommodation booking handy. Sometimes, border officials may ask for proof of onward travel or proof that you have a place to stay during your visit. Keeping these documents easily accessible can help you avoid any delays or questions when entering the country.

If you've booked through a travel agency or accommodation platform, you can typically access and print out your confirmation emails or make digital copies available on your phone. Having these details ready in advance can streamline your arrival process.

Health Documentation

In light of recent global health concerns, many countries, including the Czech Republic, have had specific health entry requirements. This might include proof of COVID-19 vaccination or a negative test result. While such requirements are constantly evolving, it's a good idea to stay up-to-date with the latest health guidelines issued by the Czech government. You can check official websites like the Czech Ministry of Foreign Affairs or consult your local embassy for the most current health and safety requirements.

If you need any specific vaccinations before traveling, it's wise to schedule those well in advance to ensure your health and safety during your trip.

Driver's License (If Renting a Car)

If you plan to rent a car during your time in Prague or anywhere else in the Czech Republic, you'll need a valid driver's license. EU citizens can use their national driver's licenses without issue, while visitors from non-EU countries might need to carry an International Driving Permit (IDP) in addition to their regular driver's license. An IDP is a translation of your license into several languages, and while not always mandatory, it's highly recommended to have one when driving abroad.

Make sure to check with your car rental company for any specific requirements regarding international driver's licenses or IDPs.

Emergency Contact Information

It's always a good idea to have a list of emergency contacts in both digital and paper form when traveling. This includes the local embassy or consulate, local emergency numbers (such as 112 for police or medical assistance), and any important contacts back home.

Having emergency information readily available can give you peace of mind in case of unexpected situations. Keep a copy of these details with you, and store another copy in a secure location, such as your hotel room, just in case.

Final Checklist for Travel Documents

Before you leave, check off the following to ensure you've covered all your essential documents:

- Valid passport (with at least six months of validity remaining)
- Visa (if required for your nationality)
- Travel insurance policy
- Flight and accommodation confirmation
- Health documentation (vaccination or test records, if needed)
- International Driving Permit (if renting a car)
- Emergency contact information

Taking the time to organize your travel documents well in advance ensures you can focus on enjoying your time in Prague, rather than scrambling to solve paperwork issues at the last minute. With the right documents in hand, you'll be ready to fully embrace the adventure that awaits you in this charming and historic city.

Navigating Czech Customs and Etiquette

Understanding Czech customs and etiquette can significantly enrich your experience in Prague. Czechs take pride in their traditions and social norms, which may differ from what you're used to in your home country. By familiarizing yourself with local customs, you'll be able to navigate social interactions with ease and show respect for the culture. Here's a closer look at the most important aspects of Czech customs and etiquette to keep in mind during your trip.

Greetings and Social Etiquette

When meeting someone in Prague, it's customary to offer a handshake, especially in formal situations. A firm, brief handshake is seen as polite, and eye contact is important during the greeting to show sincerity. While handshakes are common in professional settings, you may also notice that friends or family may greet each other with a kiss on both cheeks, but this is reserved for close relationships.

In more relaxed, casual settings, Czechs generally greet each other with "Ahoj" (ah-hoy), which is akin to saying "Hello" or "Hi." For more formal occasions, "Dobrý den" (doh-bree den) is used, which means "Good day." In Prague's cosmopolitan atmosphere, English is widely spoken, especially in tourist areas, so don't worry if you're not fluent in Czech. However, learning a few basic Czech phrases can be a nice gesture that shows respect for the local culture.

Table Manners and Dining Etiquette

Czech dining etiquette is relatively straightforward, but it's important to follow some basic rules to avoid any cultural faux pas. If you're invited to a Czech home or dining establishment, it's customary to wait for your host to begin the meal. If you're in a formal setting, a toast is often made before starting to eat. The most common phrase for a toast is "Na zdraví," which translates to "To your health."

At the table, keep your hands on the table but avoid resting your elbows. Czechs typically use utensils throughout the meal, and it's considered rude to start eating before everyone has been served. You'll often find that meals are served in courses, with soup being a common starter. If you're at a Czech home, it's polite to finish everything on your plate, as leaving food can be seen as wasteful or disrespectful.

When dining at a restaurant, it's common practice to wait for the server to bring the bill. It's also customary to leave a tip, usually around 10% of the total bill, although it's not obligatory. You can hand the tip directly to the waiter or leave it on the table when you're finished.

Personal Space and Politeness

Czechs tend to value their personal space, so be mindful of this in public spaces. It's customary to stand about an arm's length away from others, especially in queues or when conversing with strangers. Close physical contact, particularly in public, is generally avoided unless you're interacting with close friends or family.

In public transportation, such as trams or buses, it's polite to offer your seat to elderly passengers or people with disabilities. Czech society values politeness, but you may also notice that Czechs don't engage in excessive small talk with strangers, especially in public. This doesn't mean they're unfriendly—it's just a cultural preference for maintaining personal space.

Punctuality and Time Sensitivity

Czechs are generally very punctual, and arriving late to a meeting, social gathering, or dinner can be seen as disrespectful. If you're meeting someone for a professional engagement or personal gathering, make sure to arrive on time. If you're running late, it's polite to inform the person you're meeting in advance to explain the situation.

When attending social events, such as a dinner or gathering, it's expected that you arrive at the scheduled time, but not necessarily too early. In Czech culture, arriving too early can be seen as awkward, while being fashionably late is generally not the norm.

Gift Giving Etiquette

If you're invited to someone's home, bringing a small gift is a thoughtful gesture, although it's not strictly required. Common gifts include flowers, chocolates, or a bottle of wine. When gifting flowers, it's customary to present an odd number of blooms, as an even number is often reserved for funerals. If you choose to give wine, it's polite to check if your host enjoys it.

If you're traveling to Prague for a special occasion or festival, you might also consider giving a small souvenir from your home country. It's the thought that counts, and the gesture of presenting a gift will be greatly appreciated.

Dress Code and Appearance

The Czech people tend to dress neatly and conservatively, especially in formal settings. If you're visiting Prague's fine dining restaurants, theaters, or cultural institutions, it's a good idea to dress smartly. For example, wearing a nice pair of shoes and avoiding overly casual attire, such as flip-flops or shorts, is expected when attending formal events.

On the other hand, Prague is a modern city, and you'll see many people dressed casually in trendy, comfortable clothes for everyday activities. However, when it comes to cultural sites, museums, or religious locations such as Prague's churches and cathedrals, it's important to dress modestly. In places like St. Vitus Cathedral, avoid wearing clothing that exposes shoulders or legs, and take care to wear respectful attire.

Tipping and Payment Etiquette

In Prague, tipping is customary but not mandatory, especially in restaurants or cafés. A tip of around 10% is generally expected, but the quality of service will often determine the amount you give. For taxi rides, rounding up the fare is a polite way of showing appreciation for good service.

If you're paying by credit card, note that many places may not allow tips to be added to the card, so it's best to keep some cash on hand for tipping. In more touristy areas, you might find that service charges are included in your bill, but it's still a good idea to leave a small tip if you've received excellent service.

Respect for Traditions

Czechs have a deep respect for their cultural and historical traditions. When visiting sites such as Prague Castle, Old Town Square, or museums, it's important to show respect for the heritage and significance of these places. Be mindful of the quiet atmosphere in places of worship, and avoid disruptive behavior when visiting cultural sites.

By respecting the local customs and etiquette, you'll be welcomed warmly into Czech society and will be able to immerse yourself in Prague's rich and vibrant culture without any cultural misunderstandings. Simply following these straightforward guidelines will go a long way in making your visit to Prague both respectful and enjoyable.

Language Tips: Essential Czech Phrases

Although Prague is a cosmopolitan city where English is widely spoken, especially in tourist areas, learning a few basic Czech phrases can enhance your experience and help you connect with locals on a deeper level. The Czech people truly appreciate it when visitors make an effort to speak their language, even if it's just a few words. Whether you're ordering a coffee, asking for directions, or simply greeting someone, these simple phrases will not only help you navigate the city but also show respect for the Czech culture.

Here are some essential Czech phrases and tips to help you during your travels:

Basic Greetings and Polite Expressions

- **Ahoj** (ah-hoy) – Hello/Hi: A casual greeting, often used among friends or in informal settings.

- **Dobrý den** (doh-bree den) – Good day: A more formal greeting, commonly used when addressing strangers or in business situations.
- **Na shledanou** (nah-skhleh-dah-noh) – Goodbye: The most common way to say farewell.
- **Prosím** (pro-seem) – Please: Used in almost every interaction; very important for polite conversation.
- **Děkuji** (dyeh-koo-yee) – Thank you: An essential word for showing gratitude.
- **Omlouvám se** (om-loh-vahm seh) – I'm sorry: Useful in situations where you may need to apologize for a minor inconvenience.
- **Ano** (ah-no) – Yes: Used for affirmation or agreement.
- **Ne** (neh) – No: A simple, direct way to decline or disagree.

Useful Phrases for Travelers

- **Kolik to stojí?** (koh-leek toh stoh-yee) – How much does this cost?: Handy for shopping or when looking to buy something.
- **Kde je ...?** (kdeh yeh) – Where is ...?: Perfect for asking directions. You can complete the sentence with locations like "hotel" (hotel), "restaurace" (restaurant), or "toaleta" (bathroom).

- **Mluvím trochu česky.** (m-loo-veem troh-khoo ches-kee) – I speak a little Czech: A great way to show you're making an effort to speak the language, and locals will likely appreciate your attempt.
- **Pomozte mi, prosím.** (poh-mohz-teh mee, pro-seem) – Please help me: A useful phrase in case you find yourself needing assistance.
- **Mohu platit kartou?** (moh-hoo plah-teet kar-toh) – Can I pay by card?: A common question when shopping or dining.
- **Kde je nejbližší stanice metra?** (kdeh yeh nay-blee-zhee stah-nee-tseh meh-trah) – Where is the nearest metro station?: Essential for using public transportation.

Dining and Shopping

- **Jeden stůl pro dva, prosím.** (yeh-den stool proh dvah, pro-seem) – A table for two, please: Perfect for when you're sitting down at a restaurant.
- **Mohu dostat menu, prosím?** (moh-hoo doh-staht meh-noo, pro-seem) – Can I have the menu, please?: Useful when you're ready to order at a restaurant or café.
- **Máte vegetariánská jídla?** (mah-teh veh-geh-tah-ree-ahn-skah yee-dlah) – Do you have vegetarian food?: A helpful phrase for vegetarian or vegan travelers.

- **Chci zaplatit.** (h-tsee zah-pla-teet) – I want to pay: Useful when you're ready to settle your bill.
- **To je moc drahé.** (toh yeh mots drah-heh) – That's too expensive: Perfect for when you're bargaining or if something is beyond your budget.

Emergency Phrases

- **Pomoc!** (poh-mots) – Help!: A must-know word for emergencies.
- **Zavolejte pomoc!** (zah-voh-lay-teh poh-mots) – Call for help!: Another phrase that can be useful in urgent situations.
- **Jsem ztracený/ztracená.** (ysem strah-tsay-nee/strah-tsah-nah) – I'm lost: A helpful phrase if you need directions.
- **Kde je nemocnice?** (kdeh yeh neh-mots-nee-tseh) – Where is the hospital?: An important phrase in case of medical emergencies.

Czech Pronunciation Tips

- **Czech is a phonetic language**, meaning most words are pronounced as they are written, but there are some exceptions. One key thing to remember is the accent—Czech words often have accents on vowels, which change the pronunciation.

- The letter **"ř"** is unique to Czech and is pronounced somewhere between a rolled "r" and a "zh" sound. It can be tricky to master, but most locals will appreciate your efforts to say it correctly.
- **Consonant clusters** in Czech can be difficult for English speakers to pronounce. For example, "strč prst skrz krk" (meaning "put your finger through your neck") is a notoriously hard-to-pronounce phrase, but don't worry if you can't quite get it right.

When to Use English

While many people in Prague speak English, especially in areas with heavy tourist traffic, it's always polite to ask if they speak English before launching into it. You can start by saying:

- **Mluvíte anglicky?** (m-loo-veet-eh ahn-glit-skee) – Do you speak English?

If they do speak English, they'll likely respond positively, but if they don't, try to use the Czech phrases you've learned or show the phrase in written form. A smile and polite attitude always go a long way.

Final Thought: Making the Effort

Even if you only manage a few words, making the effort to speak Czech will endear you to locals and enhance your travel experience. Czechs tend to be proud of their language and culture, so showing a willingness to learn and use their language will be appreciated. Remember, the key is not perfection but making a genuine effort to connect with the people and the city. Plus, it's always fun to pick up a few new words along the way!

By incorporating these phrases into your interactions, you'll feel more confident exploring Prague and engaging with locals, allowing you to truly immerse yourself in the experience of this incredible city.

Chapter Four

Getting to and Around Prague

How to Get to Prague: Flights, Trains, and Buses

Prague, the charming capital of the Czech Republic, is easily accessible from nearly every corner of Europe and beyond. Whether you're arriving by plane, train, or bus, getting to this vibrant city is straightforward and convenient. In this section, we'll break down the various options for reaching Prague, offering you helpful tips on how to make your journey as smooth as possible.

By Air: Arriving at Václav Havel Airport

The most common way to reach Prague is by air, and the city is well-served by its international gateway, Václav Havel Airport Prague (PRG), located about 15 kilometers (9 miles) from the city center. This modern airport offers both direct and connecting flights from all over the world, making it a major entry point for international travelers.

- **Direct Flights**: Most European cities are connected to Prague with frequent direct flights. Popular airlines such as Czech Airlines, Lufthansa, Ryanair, and EasyJet fly into Prague daily, as well as many other international carriers. If you're coming from outside Europe, you can easily connect through major hubs like Frankfurt, London, or Vienna.

- **Arrival Tips**: Upon arrival, you'll find a range of services at the airport, including currency exchange, ATMs, and free Wi-Fi. If you need a SIM card or travel essentials, there are shops and kiosks in the terminals. The airport is relatively small, so it's easy to navigate.

By Train: A Scenic and Comfortable Journey

Traveling to Prague by train is a fantastic way to experience the European countryside and enjoy a comfortable, eco-friendly journey. The city is a major hub on the European rail network, and trains from neighboring countries like Austria, Germany, Poland, Slovakia, and Hungary run frequently.

- **From Within Europe**: Prague's main train station, **Praha Hlavní nádraží**, is centrally located and well-connected to various European cities. Trains from cities like Vienna, Berlin, Budapest, and Kraków are popular options for travelers coming to Prague. If you're traveling from further afield, the night trains from cities like Berlin and Vienna are a great choice, offering overnight services to maximize your travel time.
- **Booking Tickets**: Tickets for trains to Prague can be easily purchased in advance online or at

the station. For international routes, consider booking tickets through sites like **Omio**, **Trainline**, or the Czech Railways (České dráhy) website. Many European rail companies offer discounts for early bookings or travel passes that allow unlimited travel within a specific time frame.

By Bus: Budget-Friendly and Accessible

If you're looking for the most affordable option to get to Prague, buses are an excellent choice. With numerous international bus lines operating in Europe, buses can be a cost-effective alternative to trains and planes.

- **Popular Bus Companies**: Major bus companies such as **FlixBus**, **RegioJet**, and **Eurolines** operate routes to Prague from cities across Europe. These buses offer direct services from popular destinations like Berlin, Vienna, and Budapest, often at lower prices compared to flights and trains.
- **Travel Comfort**: While not as fast as flying or taking the train, buses in Europe are usually equipped with Wi-Fi, power outlets, and comfortable seating. The journey can take longer depending on where you're traveling from, but it offers an affordable and convenient option for budget travelers.

- **Booking and Timetables**: Buses can be booked online via the bus company websites or through platforms like **Busbud** and **Omio**. These sites provide easy access to timetables, routes, and prices, ensuring you find the best deal for your trip to Prague.

Combination of Travel Methods

If you're traveling from a city that doesn't have a direct connection to Prague, or if you want to explore more of the region, consider combining different transportation methods. For instance, you might take a train from one city to a larger hub like Vienna or Munich and then catch a bus or a budget flight to Prague. Many travelers opt for this combination, as it allows for flexibility and a chance to see multiple destinations along the way.

Travel Tips for a Smooth Journey

- **Travel Insurance**: Consider purchasing travel insurance that covers flight delays, cancellations, or lost luggage. It's always better to be prepared.

- **Arrival Time**: Whether arriving by plane, train, or bus, plan to arrive at your station or airport at least 30 minutes before departure, especially if you need to navigate security or ticket counters.

- **Currency and Payments**: While the Czech Republic is part of the European Union, it does not use the euro. Make sure you have some Czech koruna (CZK) for small expenses, though cards are widely accepted. You can exchange currency at the airport or withdraw cash from ATMs in Prague.

Summary: Choosing the Best Travel Option

Each mode of transport to Prague has its own advantages, depending on your time, budget, and travel preferences. Flying is the quickest and most common method, especially for international travelers. Trains provide a comfortable, scenic route, ideal for those traveling from neighboring countries. Buses are perfect for budget-conscious travelers who don't mind a longer journey. Whichever way you choose to get to Prague, you can rest assured that the city's well-connected transport network will make your arrival hassle-free.

Public Transportation: Trams, Metros, and Buses

Prague boasts an extensive and efficient public transportation network that makes getting around the city a breeze. Whether you're navigating the charming Old Town, exploring the hip neighborhoods on the outskirts, or heading to the airport, Prague's public transport system will help you reach your destination quickly and affordably. In this section, we'll guide you through the different modes of public transport in the city and how to make the most of them.

Trams: The Heart of Prague's Public Transport

Trams are an iconic part of Prague's public transportation system. With over 30 routes crisscrossing the city, they are an excellent way to explore Prague's diverse neighborhoods. Trams are often the most scenic way to travel around the city, as they pass through picturesque streets, historic squares, and along the Vltava River.

- **Why Take the Tram?**
  Trams are a great option for both tourists and locals alike, as they connect many of the city's key attractions, including Old Town, Wenceslas Square, Prague Castle, and the neighborhoods

of Vinohrady and Žižkov. If you're not in a rush, riding the tram provides a pleasant way to see more of Prague's architecture and local life.

- **Operating Hours**
  Trams run frequently from early in the morning until midnight, with night trams operating on select routes after midnight. Trams run every 5 to 10 minutes during peak hours and every 15 to 20 minutes at night.

- **How to Ride**
  Tickets for trams are the same as those used for buses and the metro (we'll explain the ticket system below). You don't need to buy a separate ticket for each tram ride. Simply board, validate your ticket, and enjoy the ride. Make sure to validate your ticket in the yellow ticket machines located near the doors of the tram.

- **Popular Tram Routes**
  - **Tram 22**: This is a must-take for first-time visitors. It passes by some of Prague's most famous sites, including the Prague Castle, the National Theatre, and the Lesser Town.
  - **Tram 17**: Known for its scenic route along the Vltava River, this tram takes you through districts like Karlín and

Holešovice, offering great views of the city.

Metro: Fast and Efficient

Prague's metro system is fast, efficient, and the most popular way for locals to travel long distances. It is divided into three lines: the green Line A, the yellow Line B, and the red Line C. These lines serve different areas of the city, connecting both the city center and the suburbs.

- **Why Take the Metro?**
  If you're in a rush or need to travel longer distances, the metro is the fastest and most convenient option. It's ideal for reaching areas that might be a bit too far for walking or when you're trying to cover a lot of ground in a short time.
- **Operating Hours**
  The metro operates from around 5:00 AM until midnight, with trains running every 2 to 4 minutes during peak times and every 6 to 10 minutes during non-peak hours.
- **How to Ride**
  Like the tram system, the metro uses a simple ticketing system. Tickets can be purchased at ticket machines or from kiosks located in metro stations. Once you have your ticket, validate it before entering the metro platform. Each line is

color-coded, making it easy to navigate. The metro stations are well-marked with clear signs in both Czech and English.

- **Popular Metro Stations**
  - **Můstek** (Line A and Line B): Located near Wenceslas Square, this station is one of the busiest and most convenient for tourists.
  - **Staroměstská** (Line A): Located in the heart of the Old Town, this station is a short walk from Prague's main attractions like Old Town Square and the Astronomical Clock.

Buses: A Practical Way to Explore the City

Buses are another crucial part of Prague's public transportation network. While trams and the metro cover most of the city's key areas, buses are essential for reaching outlying neighborhoods and destinations not served by the metro or tram lines. Buses in Prague are modern, clean, and run regularly throughout the city.

- **Why Take the Bus?**
  Buses complement the tram and metro services, filling in the gaps in areas where trains don't go, such as residential neighborhoods or remote attractions like the Prague Zoo and the Botanical Gardens. Buses are also helpful if you're traveling to the airport or taking a trip out of the city center.

- **Operating Hours**
  Similar to trams, buses operate throughout the day until midnight, with night buses running on select routes after hours. The frequency of bus services varies by route, with more popular routes operating every 10 to 15 minutes during the day and less frequent buses on evenings and weekends.

- **How to Ride**

  Bus tickets are the same as tram and metro tickets, and you must validate your ticket when boarding. Buses generally have a driver in the front, so there's no need to worry about validating your ticket at a separate machine.

- **Popular Bus Routes**

  ○ **Bus 119**: This route takes you from the airport to the metro station Nádraží Veleslavín (Line A), making it an easy and inexpensive way to get into the city center.

  ○ **Bus 207**: This bus travels from the city center to the Prague Zoo, one of the city's most beloved attractions. It's a great way to visit without worrying about taxis or long walks.

Integrated Ticket System

Prague's public transport system operates on an integrated ticketing system, which means that your ticket is valid for all modes of transport (tram, metro, and bus) within a certain time frame. You can purchase tickets for 30 minutes, 90 minutes, 1 day, or even longer. Simply board any tram, metro, or bus and validate your ticket by stamping it in the yellow machines.

- **Where to Buy Tickets**: Tickets can be purchased at ticket vending machines located at metro stations, some tram stops, or directly on buses (though only in exact change). You can also buy tickets using mobile apps like **Sejf** or **MND** for added convenience.
- **Fines and Ticket Control**: If you're caught traveling without a valid ticket, you'll face a fine. Ticket inspectors conduct random checks, so it's best to always validate your ticket to avoid any unpleasant surprises.

Final Thoughts: Navigating Prague with Ease

Prague's public transportation is reliable, affordable, and easy to navigate. Whether you're hopping on a tram to see the sights or taking the metro to reach the city's outskirts, the network is designed with both locals and tourists in mind. With frequent services and clear signage, traveling around Prague will feel effortless, allowing you to focus on enjoying the city and its many attractions. Don't forget to purchase your tickets in advance, keep your ticket validated, and take in the beautiful views along the way!

Walking and Biking in the City

Prague's charm lies in its compact, walkable layout, making it an ideal city to explore on foot or by bike. From cobbled streets in the Old Town to scenic riverside paths, the city offers countless opportunities to soak in the atmosphere, discover new corners, and enjoy a leisurely pace. Whether you prefer strolling through historical neighborhoods or cycling along the Vltava River, walking and biking are excellent ways to experience Prague like a local.

Walking: A Stroll Through History

Prague's old-world charm is best experienced on foot, as many of its iconic landmarks and hidden treasures are located close to one another. The city center is pedestrian-friendly, with narrow streets and squares perfect for leisurely exploration.

- **Explore the Old Town (Staré Město)**: The heart of Prague is filled with history, from the famous Astronomical Clock to the winding streets around Old Town Square. Walking is the best way to appreciate the detailed architecture, shop in boutique stores, or stop for a coffee at one of the cozy cafes that dot the streets.
- **Crossing the Charles Bridge**: A walk across the Charles Bridge is a must when in Prague. The bridge, one of the most famous in the world, offers breathtaking views of the city and the Vltava River. It's especially beautiful early in the morning before the crowds arrive or at sunset when the light turns golden.

- **Vinohrady and Žižkov**: These residential neighborhoods are perfect for a relaxed stroll. Vinohrady offers wide, tree-lined boulevards and beautiful parks, while Žižkov boasts quirky cafes, street art, and a more local, laid-back vibe. Both areas offer a unique glimpse into Prague's everyday life.
- **Parks and Green Spaces**: Don't miss Prague's parks and gardens, which offer peaceful retreats from the bustling city. Letná Park, with its sweeping views of the Old Town, is a favorite among locals. Petřín Hill, with its lookout tower and rose gardens, is another lovely spot to walk and take in the panorama of the city.

Biking: An Active Way to Explore

Biking is becoming increasingly popular in Prague, and for good reason. The city is gradually expanding its network of bike lanes, and there are plenty of places to rent bikes if you don't have one with you. Biking offers a fun, eco-friendly way to get around, particularly for those who want to explore farther-reaching areas of the city.

- **Bike-Friendly Areas**: Many areas in Prague, particularly along the Vltava River, are ideal for cycling. The **Vltava River Trail** is a scenic and relatively flat route that takes you along the water and through parks, offering beautiful views of Prague Castle and other landmarks. You can also cycle through **Letná Park** and along the embankment road towards **Vyšehrad**, another historic hilltop spot.

- **Bike Rental Services**: Renting a bike in Prague is easy. There are numerous bike rental shops near major tourist areas like the Old Town and the Prague Castle. Some companies even offer guided bike tours, which are a great way to learn about the city's history while cycling. If you're looking for something more casual, bike-sharing services like **Rekola** offer an affordable way to pick up and drop off bikes around the city.

- **Cycling Tours**: If you're new to the city or prefer a guided experience, there are plenty of bike tours available. These tours typically focus on the city's major landmarks but can also include off-the-beaten-path spots, like hidden courtyards and local cafes. Biking tours are a fun, interactive way to get to know the city, especially if you're traveling with a group.

- **Safety and Etiquette**: While biking in Prague is generally safe, it's important to follow local rules. Always stay on designated bike lanes when available, and be mindful of pedestrians, especially in busy areas. Helmets are not mandatory for adults, but it's always a good idea to wear one for safety. Additionally, respect the traffic signals and be aware of public transport vehicles and cars on the road.

Tips for Walking and Biking in Prague

- **Wear Comfortable Shoes**: Prague's cobbled streets, especially in the Old Town, can be uneven, so make sure to wear comfortable shoes for both walking and biking. This will ensure you can comfortably explore the city without worrying about blisters or discomfort.
- **Stay Hydrated**: Whether you're walking or biking, especially during the warmer months, it's important to stay hydrated. There are plenty of water fountains around the city,

particularly in parks, and many cafes offer water for free if you ask.

- **Weather Considerations**: Prague's weather can be unpredictable. Summers are warm but can also bring sudden rain showers, while winters can be cold and snowy. It's always good to check the weather forecast before heading out, and if you're biking, be prepared with the right clothing and gear.
- **Guided Walking Tours**: If you prefer to have some background knowledge as you explore, consider joining one of Prague's many walking tours. From historical tours to food tours, these guided walks offer an insider's perspective of the city and its rich culture.

Final Thoughts: A City Made for Walking and Biking

Prague's compact layout, beautiful scenery, and rich history make it a city made for walking and biking. Whether you're taking a leisurely stroll through the cobbled streets of Old Town or enjoying a bike ride along the Vltava River, exploring the city on foot or two wheels offers a more intimate and memorable way to discover Prague. The slower pace allows you to connect with the city in a way that public transport or taxis simply can't match. So lace up your shoes or hop on a bike—Prague is waiting for you to explore at your own pace!

Car Rentals and Taxis

While Prague is known for its excellent public transportation system, there are times when renting a car or using a taxi might be more convenient—whether for a day trip to the countryside, a late-night outing, or simply enjoying the freedom to explore at your own pace. Below, we'll take a closer look at the options for car rentals and taxis in Prague, offering insight into when they might be the best choice for your travels.

Car Rentals in Prague

Renting a car in Prague can give you a sense of independence, especially if you're planning to venture outside the city or want more flexibility during your stay. Though Prague's city center is compact and well-connected by public transport, having a car might be ideal for exploring the Czech Republic's beautiful countryside, nearby towns, or natural parks.

- **Where to Rent a Car**: There are several international and local car rental companies operating in Prague, with offices located at the airport (Václav Havel Airport) as well as in the city center. Companies like **Hertz**, **Avis**, **Sixt**, and **Europcar** offer a variety of vehicles, from economy cars to SUVs, depending on your needs. If you're planning to rent a car from the airport, booking ahead is a good idea, especially during the peak travel season.

- **Driving in Prague**: While driving in Prague itself isn't necessarily difficult, it can be challenging for first-time visitors due to narrow streets, limited parking, and traffic congestion in the city center. Most tourists prefer to use public transportation to explore Prague's top attractions. However, if you choose to rent a car, keep in mind that the roads are well-maintained and clearly marked, and Czech drivers generally follow traffic rules.

- **Parking**: Parking in Prague can be tricky, especially in the Old Town where spaces are limited and parking fees can be high. The city has several parking zones, with blue, orange, and green zones that designate where you can park. If you're renting a car, it's worth checking in advance about parking options at your accommodation or nearby parking garages. Alternatively, there are park-and-ride facilities on the outskirts of the city where you can park and take public transport into the center.

- **Driving Outside Prague**: Renting a car becomes much more useful when you're venturing outside Prague. The Czech Republic boasts scenic areas such as the **Bohemian Paradise**, **Český Krumlov**, and the **Karlovy Vary spa region**, all of which are best accessed by car. Major highways are in excellent condition, and the country is well-connected with other parts of Europe, so if you're planning a road trip, renting a car offers flexibility and comfort.

- **Renting Tips**: Be sure to have an international driver's license if you're from outside the European Union. Most car rental agencies require a valid credit card, and some may ask for an additional deposit for security. It's also advisable to purchase full insurance coverage to avoid unexpected costs. Be mindful of road signs, as some may be in Czech, and familiarize yourself with local road rules before setting out.

Taxis in Prague

Prague has a reliable and affordable taxi service, which can be an easy way to get around if you're not keen on navigating public transport or walking. Taxis are widely available in the city, and while they may not always be necessary for short distances, they can be a practical option for reaching destinations that are harder to access or when you're in a hurry.

- **How to Hail a Taxi**: You can easily find a taxi in Prague by hailing one on the street or by calling a taxi company directly. Taxis are typically black or yellow with a taxi sign on the roof. Alternatively, you can use ride-hailing apps such as **Bolt** or **Uber**, which operate in Prague and often offer slightly lower prices than traditional taxis.

- **Taxi Fares**: Prague's taxis are generally affordable, especially compared to other major European cities. The base fare is around 40 CZK, with additional charges depending on the distance traveled and the time of day. Taxis are metered, and the price should be clearly displayed on the meter during your ride. If you're concerned about potential overcharging, it's a good idea to ask the driver for an estimated fare before starting the ride.

- **Taxis from the Airport**: Taxis from Václav Havel Airport to the city center are readily available, though you should be cautious when using airport taxis. To avoid scams or overpriced fares, it's recommended to use official airport taxis or book a ride through a reliable company in advance. Some services offer fixed-price transfers to popular destinations in the city, which can be more economical and stress-free.

- **Taxis for Day Trips**: Taxis can also be a good option for short day trips or excursions around the city. For instance, if you're visiting the **Prague Castle** or going on a vineyard tour in the surrounding regions, a taxi can provide a comfortable and convenient way to get there without worrying about parking or navigating public transport.

- **Tipping**: Tipping taxi drivers in Prague is appreciated but not mandatory. A tip of 10% is standard if you're satisfied with the service, but rounding up the fare is also common practice.

Final Thoughts: Weighing Your Options

While Prague is a wonderfully walkable city with excellent public transportation, there are times when renting a car or taking a taxi is more practical. Renting a car is ideal for exploring the beautiful Czech countryside and nearby towns, while taxis provide convenience and ease of travel within the city, especially for short distances or late-night rides.

Whatever your choice, be sure to plan ahead, especially during peak tourist seasons, to ensure a smooth and enjoyable journey throughout Prague.

Chapter Five

Where to Stay in Prague

Best Neighborhoods to Stay In

Prague is a city of neighborhoods, each offering its own charm, character, and atmosphere. Whether you're a first-time visitor or a seasoned traveler, choosing the right neighborhood can make all the difference in your experience. From the historic heart of the city to trendy, residential areas, Prague has something for everyone. Here's a guide to the best neighborhoods to stay in, based on your interests, preferences, and the type of experience you're seeking.

1. Old Town (Staré Město): The Heart of Prague

For many visitors, the Old Town is the quintessential Prague experience. This is where you'll find the city's most iconic landmarks, from the **Astronomical Clock** and **Old Town Square** to the winding, cobblestone streets that exude centuries of history. Staying here places you in the heart of Prague, with easy access to most of the city's major attractions.

- **Perfect for**: First-time visitors, history lovers, culture seekers.
- **What to Expect**: A bustling, vibrant area full of shops, cafes, and restaurants, with plenty of tourists and street performers adding to the

atmosphere. You'll be within walking distance of top sites like **Prague Castle**, **Charles Bridge**, and **Wenceslas Square**. However, keep in mind that the area can be quite crowded, especially during peak seasons.

- **Why Stay Here**: If you want to experience Prague's charm in its most traditional form, Old Town is the place to be. With stunning historical buildings, a wide range of dining options, and all the major attractions at your doorstep, this area offers the best of Prague's past and present.

2. Lesser Town (Malá Strana): A Tranquil, Romantic Neighborhood

Located just across the **Vltava River** from Old Town, **Lesser Town (Malá Strana)** is one of Prague's most picturesque districts. Known for its narrow, winding streets and baroque architecture, this neighborhood has a more peaceful, romantic atmosphere compared to the bustling Old Town.

- **Perfect for**: Couples, those seeking a more relaxed vibe, history buffs.
- **What to Expect**: Lesser Town is quieter but equally beautiful, with lovely gardens, intimate cafes, and historic churches like **St. Nicholas Church**. The neighborhood is home to the majestic **Prague Castle**, which is just a short

walk away, and the beautiful **Petřín Hill** offers panoramic views of the city. It's less crowded than the Old Town but still close enough to major attractions.

- **Why Stay Here**: If you want to feel like a local while still being within walking distance of Prague's key attractions, **Lesser Town** is perfect. With its romantic ambiance, quiet charm, and stunning views, it's an ideal base for those seeking a more laid-back experience.

3. New Town (Nové Město): A Blend of Modern and Historic

New Town is another central area of Prague, but it offers a more modern feel compared to the Old Town and Lesser Town. While the **Wenceslas Square**, a bustling hub of commerce and culture, is located here, you'll also find a mix of contemporary stores, shopping centers, and vibrant nightlife.

- **Perfect for**: Shoppers, nightlife lovers, modern culture seekers.
- **What to Expect**: New Town is a lively area with wide boulevards, trendy restaurants, and contemporary art galleries. It's home to key historical sites such as the **National Museum** and **State Opera**, as well as the famous **Wenceslas Square**. New Town is more dynamic and urban, with plenty of opportunities to experience Prague's modern side.
- **Why Stay Here**: If you're interested in shopping, vibrant nightlife, and modern cultural attractions, New Town is the ideal neighborhood. You'll also find excellent transportation links, making it easy to explore other parts of Prague.

4. Vinohrady: A Trendy, Residential Area

If you're looking for a more local experience, **Vinohrady** is one of Prague's most desirable neighborhoods for residents and visitors alike. It's known for its tree-lined streets, beautiful parks, and a fantastic selection of cafes, bars, and restaurants.

- **Perfect for**: Longer stays, those seeking a quieter vibe with access to trendy spots, expats.
- **What to Expect**: Vinohrady has a relaxed, village-like atmosphere, but it's only a short tram ride away from the city center. The area is home to **Riegrovy Sady Park**, a local favorite for relaxing and picnicking, and **Jiřího z Poděbrad Square**, a lively area with markets and cafes. The neighborhood has a mix of old and new architecture, with Art Nouveau buildings and modern apartments.
- **Why Stay Here**: Vinohrady is perfect if you want to stay in a quieter, more residential part of Prague while still being close to the action. It's a great place to experience local life, with plenty of trendy bars, local markets, and green spaces for relaxing.

5. Žižkov: A Bohemian, Up-and-Coming Area

Žižkov is a lively and eclectic neighborhood that's become increasingly popular with locals and tourists alike. Known for its bohemian vibe, vibrant street art, and affordable bars, Žižkov is where you'll find a youthful and alternative side of Prague.

- **Perfect for**: Budget travelers, young people, those interested in Prague's alternative culture.
- **What to Expect**: Žižkov has a raw, gritty charm, with quirky cafes, craft beer pubs, and second-hand shops. The area is home to the **Žižkov Television Tower**, an architectural landmark that offers great views of the city. It's a lively, creative neighborhood with a unique,

offbeat character that stands in contrast to the more polished Old Town and Lesser Town.

- **Why Stay Here**: If you're looking for a more affordable place to stay and want to experience a more alternative side of Prague, Žižkov offers great options. It's a fun, youthful area that's perfect for those who like to explore off the beaten path.

6. Holešovice: The Up-and-Coming District

Holešovice is a once industrial area that has rapidly transformed into a trendy district filled with art galleries, modern cafes, and creative spaces. It's an emerging neighborhood in Prague that's gaining attention for its cultural scene and laid-back atmosphere.

- **Perfect for**: Art lovers, those seeking a unique and quiet vibe, travelers looking for an alternative to traditional tourist areas.
- **What to Expect**: Located just across the river from Old Town, Holešovice is home to the popular **DOX Centre for Contemporary Art** and many small galleries and cafes. The area also has several local markets, and it's close to **Stromovka Park**, one of Prague's largest green spaces. Holešovice offers a more local, less touristy feel while still being conveniently close to the city center.
- **Why Stay Here**: If you're an art enthusiast or someone looking for a more creative, relaxed area to stay, Holešovice is an excellent choice. It's an up-and-coming district with a unique atmosphere that's perfect for those who want to experience a different side of Prague.

Final Thoughts

Prague is a city of diverse neighborhoods, each with its own character and charm. Whether you want to stay in the historic heart of the city, enjoy the tranquility of a residential area, or explore a vibrant, bohemian neighborhood, there's a place for every type of traveler. By considering the vibe and amenities of each district, you can ensure that your stay in Prague will be memorable and perfectly suited to your style of travel.

Budget-Friendly Accommodations

Traveling to Prague on a budget doesn't mean you have to sacrifice comfort or location. The city offers a wide range of affordable accommodations that allow you to enjoy the beauty and charm of Prague without breaking the bank. Whether you're a backpacker, a student, or simply someone looking to save a little, there are plenty of options to suit your needs. From cozy hostels to budget hotels and guesthouses, here's a guide to the best budget-friendly places to stay in Prague.

1. Hostels: Affordable, Social, and Fun

Prague is well-known for its vibrant hostel scene, where you can meet fellow travelers while enjoying the city on a budget. Hostels are perfect for those seeking a social experience, with communal areas, shared kitchens, and plenty of opportunities to connect with other tourists. Many hostels also offer organized tours, pub crawls, and events, making them a great choice for younger travelers or solo adventurers.

- **What to Expect**: Expect clean, basic facilities with shared dorm rooms or private rooms at affordable prices. Some hostels also include free breakfast, Wi-Fi, and lockers for your belongings. While hostels are more basic compared to hotels, they offer excellent value for money and a lively, welcoming atmosphere.
- **Popular Options**:
  - **Czech Inn Hostel**: Located in the Vinohrady area, this modern, stylish hostel offers both dormitory-style rooms and private rooms. It's known for its great service, social vibe, and clean facilities.
  - **Hostel One Prague**: Situated near the Old Town, this popular hostel offers a

great social environment with daily events, a fully equipped kitchen, and friendly staff.

- **Why Stay Here**: If you're traveling solo or with a group of friends and want to meet people, hostels offer an affordable, social experience. They are also often located in central areas, meaning you can easily access Prague's attractions without spending too much on transportation.

2. Budget Hotels: Comfort Without the Price Tag

For those who prefer more privacy or comfort, budget hotels offer a great balance between affordability and quality. Many of these hotels are located just a short tram or metro ride from the city center, giving you easy access to Prague's key attractions without the high prices that come with staying in the Old Town.

- **What to Expect**: Budget hotels typically provide clean, comfortable rooms with private bathrooms, Wi-Fi, and basic amenities like air conditioning or breakfast. You won't get luxury service, but you will find cozy accommodations that allow you to relax after a day of sightseeing.
- **Popular Options**:

- ○ **Hotel Archibald City**: A budget hotel located in New Town, just a 10-minute walk from Wenceslas Square. It offers comfortable rooms with a hearty breakfast included and a convenient location.
- ○ **Ibis Praha Old Town**: Located near the heart of the city, this affordable hotel offers simple, modern rooms and great amenities at a reasonable price. It's perfect for those looking for comfort without spending a fortune.
- **Why Stay Here**: Budget hotels are ideal for travelers who value comfort but don't want to pay a premium for central locations. They provide good value for money and often have more privacy and quiet than hostels.

3. Guesthouses and Pensions: A Local Experience

For those looking to experience a more local, homey atmosphere, staying in a guesthouse or pension can be a wonderful choice. These smaller, family-run accommodations offer a more intimate experience compared to larger hotels and often reflect the character of the neighborhood they're in. Many guesthouses serve delicious homemade breakfasts and provide personalized service, making them a cozy and affordable option.

- **What to Expect**: Guesthouses and pensions typically offer private rooms, often with en-suite bathrooms, in a charming and welcoming environment. While they may not have all the modern luxuries of larger hotels, they make up for it with a friendly atmosphere and local charm.

- **Popular Options**:
    - ○ **Pension U Lilie**: A charming, family-run guesthouse in the Old Town. With cozy rooms, a great location, and a homemade breakfast, this pension offers a quiet retreat in the heart of the city.
    - ○ **Hotel & Residence ROYAL STANDARD**: A lovely pension in Prague's Mala Strana, offering affordable rates and personalized service in a peaceful, historic setting.
- **Why Stay Here**: If you're looking for a more personal experience and enjoy staying in smaller, local accommodations, guesthouses and pensions offer the perfect balance of affordability and character. Staying in one of these accommodations allows you to feel like a local while enjoying the comforts of home.

4. Apartments and Short-Term Rentals: Flexibility and Privacy

If you prefer more flexibility during your stay or need more space, renting an apartment or using short-term rental services like Airbnb can be an excellent budget-friendly option. Renting an apartment offers you the chance to live more like a local, with the added bonus of cooking your own meals, doing laundry, and enjoying extra space.

- **What to Expect**: Short-term rentals provide fully furnished apartments with kitchens, living areas, and private bathrooms. You'll typically have more privacy than staying in a hotel, and the ability to cook your own meals can save money, especially in a city like Prague where dining out can add up quickly.
- **Popular Options**:
  - **Airbnb**: There are many budget-friendly apartments available in various parts of the city, from small studios in New Town to larger apartments in quieter neighborhoods like Vinohrady and Žižkov.
  - **Prague City Apartments**: Located across the city, these apartments provide fully equipped living spaces at affordable prices, often with discounts for longer stays.
- **Why Stay Here**: Renting an apartment is ideal for those who want a more independent experience, with the ability to cook and live like a local. It's also perfect for families, groups, or travelers who plan to stay in Prague for more than a few nights.

5. Budget-Friendly Options Outside the City Center

While staying in the city center can be convenient, you may find better deals on accommodations in Prague's outer neighborhoods. Areas like **Vyšehrad**, **Holešovice**, and **Karlin** offer quieter, more residential environments, and they are well-connected to the city center by public transport.

- **What to Expect**: These areas offer a mix of budget hotels, pensions, and apartments at lower prices than in the city center. The accommodation quality remains high, but the atmosphere is more laid-back and local.
- **Why Stay Here**: If you're looking for a quieter stay or are traveling on a tight budget, these areas offer great value for money without compromising on convenience. With trams and metros easily accessible, you'll still be able to explore the main sights without hassle.

Final Thoughts

Prague offers a wide variety of budget-friendly accommodation options, allowing you to enjoy this beautiful city without spending a fortune. Whether you opt for a lively hostel, a cozy guesthouse, or a private apartment, you'll find plenty of ways to save on your stay while still enjoying the comfort and convenience of a great location. With thoughtful planning and a bit of research, you can easily find an affordable option that fits your travel style and ensures you have an unforgettable Prague experience.

Mid-Range Hotels and Apartments

If you're looking for a balance between comfort, convenience, and affordability, mid-range hotels and apartments in Prague are the perfect option. These accommodations offer a higher level of service and amenities than budget options, while still being reasonably priced. They are ideal for travelers who want a little more luxury and space but don't want to splurge on high-end hotels. Many of these options are located in convenient areas of the city, giving you easy access to Prague's famous attractions, while providing a more peaceful and less tourist-heavy atmosphere than the bustling city center.

1. Modern Hotels with Style and Comfort

Mid-range hotels in Prague offer comfortable rooms with modern amenities like air conditioning, free Wi-Fi, and sometimes even wellness facilities like gyms or saunas. These hotels cater to tourists who appreciate comfort and quality service without the extravagant prices of luxury hotels. Whether you're staying for a few nights or an extended vacation, you can expect well-maintained facilities, helpful staff, and a relaxing environment after a long day of sightseeing.

- **What to Expect**: Rooms in mid-range hotels often feature stylish decor, larger beds, flat-screen TVs, minibars, and sometimes even small kitchenettes. Many hotels also offer complimentary breakfast or access to a buffet, making it easier to start your day before heading out to explore.

- **Popular Options**:
    - **Hotel Julian**: Located in the Mala Strana district, just a short walk from Charles Bridge, Hotel Julian offers modern rooms with fantastic views over the city and a wellness center for a relaxing stay.
    - **Hotel Mysterius**: A stylish boutique hotel near Wenceslas Square, it combines contemporary comfort with traditional Prague charm, offering spacious rooms and a variety of services at an affordable price.
- **Why Stay Here**: These hotels provide an excellent combination of service, quality, and price. Whether you're visiting for business or pleasure, the amenities and location will help make your stay as enjoyable and stress-free as possible.

2. Apartment Stays: Flexibility and Space

For travelers who want more independence and space, renting a mid-range apartment in Prague can be an excellent option. Apartments are a great choice for families, small groups, or those planning a longer stay. With private kitchen facilities, living areas, and separate bedrooms, these accommodations allow you to enjoy the city with more freedom and comfort. Whether you're looking for a cozy studio or a spacious multi-bedroom apartment, there's a wide range of options available to suit your needs.

- **What to Expect**: Apartments often come with a fully equipped kitchen, meaning you can prepare your own meals and save money on dining out. Many are also located in central neighborhoods like Old Town, Vinohrady, and New Town, putting you within walking distance of major attractions, or close to public transport for easy access to the city center.

- **Popular Options**:
  - **Prague City Apartments**: A well-regarded provider of mid-range rentals, offering apartments throughout Prague, from contemporary studios to larger family-sized spaces. Expect fully furnished apartments with all the comforts of home, including free Wi-Fi and washing facilities.
  - **Old Town Apartments**: Located in the heart of Prague, these apartments offer a combination of traditional and modern elements. The spacious apartments come with kitchenettes, making them a great choice for those who prefer to prepare their own meals.
- **Why Stay Here**: Renting an apartment offers more flexibility than staying in a hotel. You'll have access to local grocery stores and markets, the freedom to cook your own meals, and the comfort of your own space. This can be particularly useful for families or groups traveling together.

3. Ideal Locations Near Prague's Best Sights

Mid-range hotels and apartments are often located in great neighborhoods that offer easy access to Prague's key sights, yet are slightly removed from the tourist crowds in the city center. Staying in areas like **Vinohrady**, **Žižkov**, or **Karlín** will give you a more authentic experience of the city while still keeping you close to popular attractions.

- **What to Expect**: These neighborhoods have plenty of cafes, restaurants, and local shops, allowing you to experience Prague's daily life. Public transportation, including metro and trams, is easily accessible from most mid-range accommodations, so you won't have any trouble getting to popular destinations like Prague Castle, Old Town Square, and the Charles Bridge.
- **Why Stay Here**: These areas tend to be quieter and more residential, offering a chance to escape the tourist hustle while being well-connected to the rest of the city. You'll enjoy both the local vibe and the convenience of having Prague's attractions within easy reach.

4. Additional Amenities for Comfort

Many mid-range hotels and apartments go the extra mile to enhance your stay by offering additional amenities and services. Whether it's a hotel that offers airport transfers, a restaurant serving local Czech cuisine, or an apartment with a private balcony overlooking the city, these added touches make your experience feel more comfortable and special.

- **What to Expect**: Some mid-range hotels may also offer wellness facilities, such as massage services or saunas, and others may have a small fitness center or a bar/lounge area where you can unwind after a day of sightseeing. Apartments may include perks like free parking, private terraces, or even laundry facilities.

- **Popular Options**:
  - **Hotel Czech Inn**: This boutique hotel in the Vinohrady district is known for its elegant design and top-notch service, offering a variety of room types and access to a fitness center, bar, and excellent breakfast options.
  - **Residence Karolina**: Located near the city center, Residence Karolina is an excellent option for travelers looking for apartment-style accommodations, with kitchenettes, laundry services, and modern amenities.
- **Why Stay Here**: These added services and amenities enhance the convenience and comfort of your stay, helping to create a relaxing and stress-free experience. Whether it's enjoying a delicious meal or taking advantage of an on-site spa, mid-range accommodations offer everything you need to unwind after a busy day of exploring.

Final Thoughts

Mid-range hotels and apartments in Prague provide the perfect balance of value, comfort, and convenience. Whether you prefer the privacy and flexibility of an apartment or the full-service experience of a hotel, these options offer a fantastic base from which to explore the city. With modern amenities, ideal locations, and the option to experience both local culture and tourist attractions, mid-range accommodations are a great choice for those seeking a comfortable yet affordable stay in one of Europe's most enchanting cities.

Luxury Stays for a Lavish Experience

For those seeking the ultimate in comfort, service, and sophistication, Prague offers a range of luxury accommodations that cater to every need. Whether you're planning a special celebration, enjoying a romantic getaway, or simply want to experience the best the city has to offer, Prague's luxury hotels provide world-class service, elegant decor, and prime locations. These stays promise an unforgettable experience, combining historical grandeur with modern amenities, and offering a level of indulgence that elevates your visit to an entirely new level.

1. Opulent Hotels with a Rich History

Many of Prague's luxury hotels are housed in historical buildings that seamlessly blend the city's rich past with modern-day elegance. These hotels exude old-world charm with high ceilings, intricate architecture, and lavish interiors, making you feel like you've stepped into a grand royal residence. But beyond their beauty, they also offer top-tier services and facilities that ensure your stay is nothing short of exceptional.

- **What to Expect**: From sumptuous rooms with stunning views to personalized services like private butlers, luxury hotels in Prague focus on providing an unparalleled level of comfort. You can expect premium bedding, marble bathrooms, gourmet dining, and exclusive spa treatments to make your stay feel truly indulgent.

- **Popular Options**:
  - **Four Seasons Hotel Prague**: One of the most famous luxury hotels in the city, the Four Seasons offers a spectacular location along the Vltava River with views of Prague Castle. Its elegant rooms, exceptional spa, and fine dining options create a lavish experience for any guest.
  - **The Augustine, a Luxury Collection Hotel**: Set in a beautifully restored monastery, this 5-star hotel combines history with contemporary luxury. With a renowned spa, exquisite dining, and an outstanding location in the Lesser Town, it offers an escape into pure luxury.
- **Why Stay Here**: These historic luxury hotels let you indulge in the grandeur of Prague's royal past while offering the best of modern hospitality. They provide a blend of comfort, class, and culture that will make your stay feel like a personal celebration.

2. Unmatched Service and Exclusive Experiences

When it comes to luxury, service is everything. In Prague's top-tier hotels, every guest is treated like royalty, with staff who go above and beyond to cater to your every need. Whether it's arranging private tours of Prague's famous sites, securing tickets for exclusive events, or arranging a gourmet meal in the comfort of your room, luxury hotels in Prague ensure that your experience is seamless and unforgettable.

- **What to Expect**: Personalized concierge services, private airport transfers, and the option to book private guides or chauffeurs are just the beginning. Many luxury hotels also offer exclusive experiences such as cooking classes, wine tastings, or even private shopping tours with personal stylists.

- **Popular Options**:
  - ○ **Mandarin Oriental Prague**: Nestled in the historic district of Mala Strana, this luxury hotel offers a tranquil retreat with a world-class spa, gourmet restaurants, and rooms designed for ultimate relaxation. The Mandarin's attention to detail, along with personalized services like yoga sessions or private cooking classes, sets it apart.
  - ○ **The Grand Mark Prague**: With its stunning courtyard garden and spacious rooms, The Grand Mark is a symbol of luxury. This hotel is known for offering VIP experiences, including private boat rides on the Vltava River and private tours of art galleries and museums.
- **Why Stay Here**: Luxury stays in Prague offer experiences that go beyond what you'd expect in a typical hotel. Whether you're enjoying a Michelin-starred meal, relaxing in an award-winning spa, or receiving personalized services, you'll feel pampered from start to finish.

3. Spa Retreats for Ultimate Relaxation

For travelers looking to unwind and recharge, Prague's luxury hotels often include world-class spas that offer a serene escape from the bustling city. After a day of sightseeing, you can indulge in a rejuvenating massage, soak in a luxurious pool, or enjoy a beauty treatment tailored to your needs. These spas focus on providing a holistic experience designed to nurture both body and soul.

- **What to Expect**: High-end spa services such as deep tissue massages, facials, aromatherapy, and therapeutic treatments are commonly available at luxury hotels. Many also offer exclusive wellness packages that include full-day experiences with access to saunas, pools, and hot tubs, often in a tranquil, secluded environment.
- **Popular Options**:
  - **Alchymist Grand Hotel and Spa**: Located in a historic building near Prague Castle, the Alchymist is known for its luxurious spa services, including exclusive massages and health treatments. The spa, housed in a former chapel, provides an intimate and relaxing setting.
  - **The Boscolo Prague**: This 5-star hotel features a sophisticated wellness center with a range of treatments, from beauty

therapies to traditional Czech spa experiences. It's a perfect place to relax after a day of exploring the city.

- **Why Stay Here**: After a day of exploring the city's attractions, retreating to a luxury hotel with spa facilities allows you to unwind and enjoy the ultimate pampering. These wellness offerings transform a simple stay into a fully rejuvenating experience.

4. Exceptional Dining and Culinary Delights

Luxury hotels in Prague often feature some of the best dining experiences the city has to offer. Whether you're in the mood for traditional Czech cuisine or international fine dining, you'll find restaurants within these hotels that offer exquisite dishes prepared by renowned chefs. Many also provide private dining options, creating intimate, unforgettable meals in stunning settings.

- **What to Expect**: Gourmet restaurants, private wine cellars, rooftop terraces with panoramic views, and bespoke dining experiences are some of the highlights of Prague's luxury hotel offerings. A stay in these hotels can be a culinary adventure as much as a journey through the city.
- **Popular Options**:
  - **La Finestra in Cucina** (at the Four Seasons): A Michelin-starred restaurant offering exceptional Italian and Czech fusion cuisine. It's an elegant and memorable dining experience, perfect for food enthusiasts.
  - **Terasa U Zlaté Studně** (at The Augustine): Located on the roof of the hotel, this restaurant offers spectacular views of Prague and serves contemporary Czech dishes with a modern twist.
- **Why Stay Here**: For food lovers, these luxury hotels provide the best of both local and international flavors, offering an unforgettable

culinary journey that adds a touch of sophistication to your Prague experience.

5. Prime Locations for a Luxurious Stay

The prime locations of Prague's luxury hotels are another reason why they stand out. Many are situated near Prague's most iconic landmarks, such as Prague Castle, Old Town Square, or the Charles Bridge. Staying in these locations not only gives you easy access to Prague's main attractions but also allows you to experience the city in all its historic glory, with views of the Vltava River or charming cobblestone streets.

- **What to Expect**: Whether you're staying in the heart of Old Town or enjoying panoramic views of the city from the comfort of your room, luxury hotels place you right in the middle of all the action, allowing you to explore Prague in style and comfort.
- **Why Stay Here**: These prime locations allow you to make the most of your visit, with major sights just a short walk away, but also provide the quiet, private retreats needed to relax after a busy day.

Final Thoughts

A luxury stay in Prague isn't just about the accommodation—it's about indulging in a complete experience that combines exceptional service, elegant surroundings, and access to exclusive experiences. From historic hotels with royal charm to modern, high-end retreats offering indulgent wellness treatments, the luxury accommodations in Prague cater to those looking to enjoy the city in style. Whether it's the exquisite dining, the serene spa, or the impeccable service, a stay at one of these hotels promises to be a lavish and memorable part of your Prague adventure.

Chapter Six

Exploring Prague's Must-See Attractions

Prague Castle: A Step into Royalty

Perched atop a hill overlooking the city, **Prague Castle (Pražský hrad)** is not just an architectural marvel but also the beating heart of the Czech Republic's history, culture, and identity. Spanning an area of over 70,000 square meters, this magnificent complex holds the title of the largest ancient castle in the world. Walking through its gates is like stepping into a living museum, where every building and courtyard tells a story of royalty, religion, and resilience.

A Historical Icon

Prague Castle has stood as a symbol of Czech statehood for over 1,000 years. Established in the 9th century, it evolved over centuries, blending Romanesque, Gothic, Renaissance, and Baroque styles. It served as the residence for Czech kings, Holy Roman Emperors, and now the President of the Czech Republic. The castle has witnessed coronations, invasions, and revolutions, making it a centerpiece of the nation's turbulent history.

Exploring the Castle Complex

The castle isn't a single building but a sprawling complex of palaces, churches, gardens, and fortifications. Here are some of its key highlights:

- **St. Vitus Cathedral**: The crown jewel of the castle complex, this Gothic masterpiece dominates the skyline and houses the tombs of Bohemian kings and the priceless Crown Jewels.
- **Old Royal Palace**: A historic residence featuring the Vladislav Hall, known for its remarkable ribbed vaulting.
- **Golden Lane**: A charming street of colorful, tiny houses once home to castle guards and artisans.
- **St. George's Basilica**: A Romanesque gem with a serene atmosphere and remarkable frescoes.
- **Castle Gardens**: Beautifully landscaped spaces offering breathtaking views of the city below.

Each corner of the castle invites exploration, from its art-filled galleries to its quiet courtyards.

Practical Information for Visitors

- **Opening Hours**:
  - The castle complex is open daily, though specific buildings have varying hours. Generally, the summer season (April to October) sees extended hours, while the winter season (November to March) has shorter days.
  - St. Vitus Cathedral, a must-see, opens earlier than other sections, so plan accordingly to avoid crowds.
- **Tickets and Pricing**:
  - Tickets are required to access the main buildings and exhibitions. They come in several packages, with the "Circuit B" ticket being the most popular, covering the Old Royal Palace, St. Vitus Cathedral, Golden Lane, and St. George's Basilica.
  - Discounts are available for children, students, and seniors. Consider purchasing your tickets online to skip the lines.
- **Getting There**:
  - The castle is easily accessible by tram. Take tram number 22 to the "Pražský hrad" stop for a direct route. Alternatively, a leisurely walk up the Old

Castle Stairs offers a scenic, albeit steep, climb.

- **When to Visit**:
  - Arrive early in the morning or late in the afternoon to avoid peak crowds. Sunset visits are particularly magical, as the castle takes on a golden hue and the city below sparkles with lights.

Insider Tips for Your Visit

1. **Plan for Time**: The castle complex is vast, so allocate at least half a day to explore thoroughly. If you're short on time, prioritize St. Vitus Cathedral and the Golden Lane.

2. **Wear Comfortable Shoes**: The cobblestone pathways and uneven surfaces can be hard on your feet, so sturdy footwear is a must.
3. **Attend the Changing of the Guard**: The ceremonial changing of the guard takes place hourly at the castle gates, with a more elaborate version at noon. It's a fascinating tradition to witness.
4. **Bring a Camera**: The views from the castle gardens and terraces are some of the best in Prague, offering perfect photo opportunities of the Vltava River, Charles Bridge, and Old Town.
5. **Look for Hidden Details**: Don't miss the intricate mosaics on the façade of St. Vitus Cathedral or the tiny exhibits in the Golden Lane houses, showcasing medieval life.

Why Visit Prague Castle?

Prague Castle isn't just a destination; it's a journey through time. From its grand halls to its serene gardens, every corner immerses you in the legacy of a city that has been a crossroads of cultures and empires. Whether you're a history enthusiast, an architecture lover, or simply someone looking for awe-inspiring views, Prague Castle promises an experience that lingers long after you leave.

Take your time to savor this treasure of Prague, and let its rich history and timeless beauty captivate you.

Charles Bridge: An Icon of the City

Stretching gracefully over the Vltava River, **Charles Bridge (Karlův most)** is one of Prague's most cherished landmarks. This stunning medieval structure, adorned with statues and steeped in history, is not just a way to get from Old Town to Prague Castle; it's a journey into the soul of the city. Whether bathed in the golden light of dawn or bustling with energy in the afternoon, Charles Bridge is a place where past and present blend seamlessly.

A Bridge Built to Last

Commissioned by King Charles IV in 1357, Charles Bridge replaced the older Judith Bridge, which had been destroyed by floods. The bridge's construction was overseen by the renowned architect Peter Parler, who also contributed to St. Vitus Cathedral. Built using sandstone and fortified with a unique mixture of egg yolks in its mortar, the bridge has withstood centuries of wear, floods, and countless footsteps.

Spanning 516 meters in length and nearly 10 meters in width, Charles Bridge connects the Old Town (Staré Město) with the Lesser Town (Malá Strana). Its 16 arches are supported by robust pillars, ensuring its durability through the ages.

Statues and Stories

One of the most enchanting aspects of Charles Bridge is its collection of 30 statues and sculptures, added in the 17th and 18th centuries. These Baroque masterpieces depict saints, historical figures, and religious scenes, each with its own story to tell.

Among the most notable is the statue of **St. John of Nepomuk**, a national saint of Bohemia. Legend has it that touching the plaque at the base of his statue brings good luck and ensures a return trip to Prague. Keep an eye out for the unique composition of statues like the dramatic depiction of **St. Luthgard** or the somber **Crucifixion of Christ**—each offers a glimpse into the artistic and spiritual heritage of the city.

Practical Information for Visitors

- **Best Times to Visit**:
    - To experience the bridge at its most tranquil, visit early in the morning or late in the evening. Sunrise offers a serene ambiance, while evening strolls reveal the illuminated cityscape.
    - Avoid midday if you prefer quieter moments, as this is when the bridge tends to be busiest with tourists, street performers, and vendors.

- **Getting There**:
  - Charles Bridge is located in the heart of Prague, easily accessible by foot from Old Town Square or Prague Castle. Tram stops like Malostranské náměstí (Lesser Town Square) or Staroměstská (Old Town) are also nearby.
- **What to Bring**:
  - Bring your camera or smartphone for photos, as the views from the bridge are breathtaking. It's an ideal spot for capturing the beauty of Prague's skyline, including the iconic Prague Castle.

Insider Tips for Exploring Charles Bridge

1. **Enjoy the Views**: Stand in the center of the bridge to take in sweeping views of the riverbanks, with Prague Castle on one side and Old Town on the other.
2. **Appreciate the Details**: Take your time to observe the intricate details of the statues. Each one tells a story, and you'll notice new things with every visit.
3. **Listen to Street Performers**: Musicians, painters, and entertainers often grace the bridge, adding a lively and artistic vibe to your stroll.
4. **Be Mindful of Pickpockets**: Like any popular tourist spot, Charles Bridge can attract

pickpockets. Keep an eye on your belongings, especially during busy times.

5. **Visit Nearby Landmarks**: On the Old Town side, the Gothic **Old Town Bridge Tower** offers a climbable vantage point with panoramic views. On the Lesser Town side, the **Lesser Town Bridge Tower** serves as a gateway to Malá Strana's charming streets.

A Symbol of Prague's Spirit

Charles Bridge is more than a historical relic; it's a living testament to Prague's resilience and creativity. Crossing the bridge feels like stepping into a postcard, with the sound of the Vltava's gentle flow beneath you and the city's vibrant life around you.

Whether you're here for the history, the art, or simply a quiet moment to reflect, Charles Bridge will leave an indelible mark on your journey through Prague. Take your time, let its beauty sink in, and allow yourself to be swept away by its timeless charm.

Old Town Square and the Astronomical Clock

In the heart of Prague's historic center lies **Old Town Square (Staroměstské náměstí)**, a vibrant gathering place that has witnessed centuries of history, celebration, and revolution. Framed by a stunning mix of Gothic, Baroque, and Romanesque architecture, the square is a must-see for anyone exploring Prague. Among its many treasures, the **Astronomical Clock (Orloj)** stands out as a marvel of medieval engineering and artistic brilliance.

A Square with Centuries of History

Dating back to the 12th century, Old Town Square has long been a focal point of Prague's political, cultural, and social life. Originally a bustling marketplace, the square evolved into a stage for momentous historical events, including the execution of 27 Czech noblemen in 1621 and key moments in the Velvet Revolution of 1989. Today, it serves as a vibrant meeting point for locals and visitors alike, offering a front-row seat to the city's unique blend of past and present.

What to See in Old Town Square

The square is more than just an open space; it's a gallery of architectural and cultural wonders.

139

- **The Gothic Church of Our Lady Before Týn**:
  With its twin spires rising dramatically against the sky, this iconic church dominates the square. Step inside to admire its stunning interior, including an ornate altar and historical relics.
- **St. Nicholas Church**:
  A masterpiece of Baroque architecture, St. Nicholas Church enchants visitors with its elegant façade and dazzling frescoes.
- **The Jan Hus Memorial**:
  This imposing statue honors the legacy of Jan Hus, a Czech religious reformer and national hero. It's a reminder of the city's spirit of resilience and reform.

The Astronomical Clock: A Medieval Marvel

Installed in 1410, the **Prague Astronomical Clock** is the third-oldest clock of its kind in the world and the oldest still in operation. Located on the southern wall of the Old Town Hall, this intricate timepiece is a blend of art, science, and storytelling.

- **The Mechanics of Time**:
  The clock doesn't just tell the hour; it displays the position of the sun and moon, the zodiac, and even the phases of the moon. Its detailed

dials and celestial mechanics are a testament to medieval craftsmanship.

- **The Hourly Show**:
Every hour, the clock springs to life in a delightful show known as "The Walk of the Apostles." As bells chime, small windows open, and a procession of wooden apostles passes by. Accompanying the figures are symbolic characters like Vanity, Greed, and Death, each moving in a carefully choreographed sequence. The show ends with a golden rooster crowing and a toll of the bell, drawing applause from onlookers.

Practical Tips for Visiting

- **Timing**:
Arrive early to secure a good viewing spot for the clock's hourly performance, especially during peak tourist seasons.
- **Climbing the Old Town Hall Tower**:
For a panoramic view of the square and beyond, climb the Old Town Hall Tower. The vista is especially magical at sunset or during the holiday season when the square is lit up with festive lights.
- **Events and Festivities**:
The square comes alive during seasonal events like Christmas and Easter markets, featuring

local crafts, traditional foods, and performances.

Insider Tips

1. **Visit Early or Late**: To avoid crowds, explore the square in the early morning or late evening when it feels more intimate.
2. **Explore Side Streets**: The streets branching off from the square are lined with hidden treasures, from boutique shops to charming cafes.
3. **Stay Alert**: Like any busy tourist spot, the square can attract pickpockets. Keep your belongings secure.

4. **Local Food Stalls**: Try traditional Czech treats like **trdelník** (chimney cake) or roasted sausages from vendors during festive markets.

A Place to Pause and Reflect

Old Town Square and the Astronomical Clock capture the essence of Prague—a city that cherishes its history while embracing modern life. Standing in the square, you can feel the weight of the centuries, the buzz of today, and the promise of tomorrow. Take a moment to soak in the energy, marvel at the architecture, and let yourself be carried away by the magic of this timeless place.

St. Vitus Cathedral: Gothic Masterpiece

Rising majestically within the grounds of **Prague Castle**, St. Vitus Cathedral is a masterpiece of Gothic architecture and one of Prague's most iconic landmarks. Its towering spires, intricate stone carvings, and vibrant stained-glass windows captivate visitors from the moment they arrive. More than just a religious site, the cathedral is a treasure trove of history, art, and spirituality, making it a must-visit for anyone exploring Prague.

A Cathedral Steeped in History

Construction of St. Vitus Cathedral began in 1344 under the direction of Charles IV, the Holy Roman Emperor and King of Bohemia. The project spanned nearly six centuries, finally completed in 1929. The cathedral has witnessed coronations of Czech kings and queens, housed the remains of saints and royals, and served as a symbol of the nation's faith and resilience.

Architectural Marvel

St. Vitus Cathedral exemplifies the grandeur of Gothic design, with elements that evoke both awe and wonder.

- **The Facade**:
  The western facade, adorned with twin spires and detailed stonework, sets the tone for the magnificence within. Look closely to appreciate the sculpted figures and ornamental gargoyles.
- **The Great South Tower**:
  This towering structure, over 96 meters tall, offers breathtaking views of the city. Climbing its 287 steps rewards visitors with an unforgettable perspective of Prague's skyline.
- **Stained-Glass Windows**:
  The vibrant stained-glass windows, including works by Czech artist Alfons Mucha, depict biblical scenes and Czech saints in dazzling detail. They bathe the interior in a kaleidoscope of colors, creating an almost ethereal atmosphere.

Highlights Inside the Cathedral

The interior of St. Vitus Cathedral is just as impressive as its exterior, filled with historical and artistic treasures.

- **The Chapel of St. Wenceslas**:
  Dedicated to the patron saint of Bohemia, this richly decorated chapel houses the saint's tomb and features stunning frescoes and semi-precious stone inlays.
- **The Royal Mausoleum and Crypt**:
  Beneath the cathedral lies the final resting place of Czech kings and queens, including Charles IV.

- **The Crown Chamber**:
  This secure chamber contains the Bohemian Crown Jewels, a symbol of Czech sovereignty. Although the jewels are rarely displayed, their presence adds to the cathedral's significance.

Practical Information for Visitors

- **Location**:
  St. Vitus Cathedral is located within Prague Castle, so your visit can easily include both landmarks.
- **Opening Hours**:
  The cathedral is open daily, but hours vary seasonally. Plan to visit early in the day to avoid crowds.
- **Tickets**:
  Entry to the cathedral is included in most Prague Castle ticket options. For a more in-depth experience, consider a guided tour that covers both the cathedral and castle grounds.

Insider Tips

1. **Explore the Exterior First**: Take time to admire the gargoyles and spires before heading inside. A good photo opportunity awaits in the castle courtyard.
2. **Climb the South Tower**: While the ascent is challenging, the view from the top is worth every step. Bring a camera!
3. **Visit During Off-Peak Hours**: Early mornings or late afternoons provide a quieter experience, allowing you to soak in the atmosphere without the crowds.
4. **Check for Special Events**: The cathedral occasionally hosts concerts and religious

ceremonies, offering a unique way to experience its grandeur.

A Spiritual and Artistic Journey

St. Vitus Cathedral is more than a building it's a living testament to Prague's history, faith, and artistry. Whether you're drawn to its architectural brilliance, historical significance, or spiritual atmosphere, this cathedral promises an experience that lingers long after you've left. Take your time to explore its many facets and let the timeless beauty of St. Vitus leave an indelible mark on your Prague journey.

The Jewish Quarter: History and Heritage

Nestled between Old Town and the Vltava River, Prague's Jewish Quarter, or Josefov, stands as a poignant testament to centuries of Jewish history, culture, and resilience. Named after Emperor Joseph II, whose reforms aimed to integrate Jewish communities into society, Josefov holds a rich yet somber past. Walking through this historic district offers a chance to reflect on the profound impact of the Jewish community on Prague's identity.

A Journey Through Time

The history of the Jewish Quarter dates back to the 10th century when Jewish merchants and settlers established a community in Prague. Over the centuries, the area endured periods of persecution, segregation, and destruction, culminating in the devastating impact of the Holocaust. Yet, Josefov also tells a story of cultural vibrancy, intellectual achievements, and the enduring spirit of its people.

Key Sites to Explore

- **Old-New Synagogue (Staronová Synagoga)**
  Built in the 13th century, the Old-New Synagogue is one of Europe's oldest active synagogues. Its simple Gothic architecture belies its spiritual significance. According to legend, the synagogue's attic is where the Golem, a mythical clay figure created by Rabbi Judah Loew to protect Prague's Jews, resides to this day.
- **Jewish Cemetery**
  One of the most evocative sites in the Jewish Quarter, the Old Jewish Cemetery is a maze of tilted gravestones marking the resting place of over 12,000 individuals. Due to space constraints, graves were layered atop one

another, creating a hauntingly beautiful landscape.

- **Jewish Museum**
  The Jewish Museum in Prague manages several important buildings and collections in Josefov. It offers a deeply moving insight into Jewish history, from religious artifacts to personal stories of those who lived through the Holocaust.

- **Pinkas Synagogue**
  This synagogue now serves as a memorial to the Czech Jews who perished in the Holocaust. The names of nearly 80,000 victims are inscribed on its walls, accompanied by an exhibit of children's drawings from the Terezín concentration camp.

- **Spanish Synagogue**
  Renowned for its stunning Moorish Revival architecture and ornate interiors, the Spanish Synagogue is a must-visit. It also hosts exhibitions on Jewish history and culture, as well as occasional concerts.

Understanding the Heritage

Prague's Jewish Quarter is more than a collection of historic sites; it is a living chronicle of a community that contributed significantly to the city's intellectual, cultural, and economic life. Figures like Franz Kafka, whose works continue to shape literary thought, emerged from this community. The area's preservation stands as a commitment to remembering the past and honoring those who shaped it.

Practical Information for Visitors

- **Location**:
  Josefov is conveniently located near Old Town Square, making it easy to include in a day of sightseeing.
- **Tickets**:
  A single ticket grants access to many of the Jewish Quarter's key sites, including synagogues and the cemetery. You can purchase it online or at the Jewish Museum.

- **Opening Hours**:
  Most sites are closed on Saturdays and Jewish holidays, so plan accordingly.

Insider Tips

1. **Take a Guided Tour**: While self-guided exploration is possible, a knowledgeable guide can provide deeper context and bring the history to life.
2. **Wear Comfortable Shoes**: The cobblestone streets can be uneven, so comfortable footwear is a must.
3. **Visit Early or Late**: Arriving early in the morning or late in the afternoon can help you avoid peak crowds.
4. **Reflect Respectfully**: Many sites, particularly the cemetery and Holocaust memorial, carry profound emotional weight. Be mindful of the solemnity of these places.

A Testament to Resilience

Visiting the Jewish Quarter is a deeply moving experience that bridges Prague's past and present. It offers a window into the Jewish community's enduring spirit and the challenges they overcame. As you explore Josefov, you'll walk away with a greater appreciation of Prague's multifaceted history and the contributions of a community that has left an indelible mark on the city's soul.

Chapter Seven

Hidden Corners and Lesser-Known Gems

Off-the-Beaten-Path Neighborhoods

While Prague's famous attractions like Old Town Square and Charles Bridge deserve the spotlight, the city is also home to charming neighborhoods that offer a more intimate look at local life. These areas are perfect for those seeking quieter streets, authentic experiences, and a glimpse into the everyday rhythm of Prague beyond the tourist trail.

1. Vršovice: A Trendy Local Haven

Once overlooked, Vršovice has blossomed into a vibrant district loved by locals. This neighborhood offers a mix of artistic vibes, green spaces, and unique cafes.

- **Why Visit**: Wander Krymská Street, lined with independent boutiques, art galleries, and coffee shops. It's a hub for Prague's creative community.

- **Don't Miss**: The Havlíčkovy Sady Park, a peaceful escape with a vineyard, a neo-Renaissance villa, and scenic views of the city.

2. Holešovice: Industrial Charm Meets Modern Art

Nestled along the Vltava River, Holešovice was once an industrial hub. Today, it's a cultural hotspot filled with galleries, design studios, and trendy eateries.

- **Why Visit**: Discover DOX Centre for Contemporary Art, a striking space for avant-garde exhibitions. Stroll through the farmers' market at Prague Market for local produce and unique souvenirs.
- **Don't Miss**: Letná Park, a sprawling green space perfect for picnics and panoramic views of Prague.

3. Karlín: Where Modern Meets Historic

After a transformative revival, Karlín has become one of Prague's most stylish neighborhoods. Its blend of historic architecture and modern developments creates a dynamic atmosphere.

- **Why Visit**: Enjoy the vibrant restaurant scene and live music venues. Explore the neighborhood's grand buildings and hidden courtyards.
- **Don't Miss**: The Church of Saints Cyril and Methodius, a neo-Romanesque gem, and the outdoor spaces of Karlínské náměstí.

4. Žižkov: A Bohemian Spirit

Known for its edgy vibe and rich history, Žižkov is Prague's bohemian quarter. Its quirky charm and vibrant nightlife make it a favorite among locals.

- **Why Visit**: Enjoy the lively bar scene or take a quiet walk up to Vítkov Hill for breathtaking city views.
- **Don't Miss**: The Žižkov Television Tower, not just for its striking architecture but also for the observation deck that offers a bird's-eye view of Prague.

5. Vyšehrad: Myth and Majesty

South of the city center, Vyšehrad offers a mix of historical intrigue and tranquil beauty. This hilltop fortress is said to be one of the oldest parts of Prague.

- **Why Visit**: Explore the ancient fortifications, the Basilica of St. Peter and St. Paul, and the serene Vyšehrad Cemetery, the final resting place of many Czech luminaries.
- **Don't Miss**: The views of the Vltava River from the ramparts are among the most romantic in Prague.

Practical Tips for Exploring Neighborhoods

- **Timing**: Early mornings or weekdays are ideal to experience these areas at their most authentic.
- **Getting Around**: Use Prague's efficient tram system or consider renting a bike for a leisurely exploration.

- **Local Etiquette**: While these neighborhoods are less touristy, it's important to respect the quiet charm and local life they represent.

Discover Prague Through Its Neighborhoods

Diving into Prague's lesser-known neighborhoods is like uncovering another layer of the city's soul. These areas are not just destinations but experiences, revealing the artistry, resilience, and daily life that make Prague unique. Whether it's sipping coffee on a quiet street or admiring the subtle beauty of an old building, these neighborhoods invite you to see Prague in a way that feels deeply personal.

Secret Gardens and Quiet Spots

Amid Prague's historic grandeur and bustling streets, the city harbors pockets of serenity where time slows down. These hidden gardens and tranquil corners offer a peaceful retreat, allowing you to reconnect with nature and reflect on your journey. Whether you're seeking a romantic setting or a quiet escape, these lesser-known spots are worth exploring.

1. Vojanovy Sady: A Hidden Oasis

Tucked away in the heart of Prague's Mala Strana district, Vojanovy Sady is one of the city's oldest gardens. Enclosed by high walls, it feels like a secret world far removed from the urban hustle.

- **Why Visit**: Wander through blooming orchards, manicured lawns, and ancient trees. Spot the resident peacocks adding a touch of elegance to the peaceful setting.
- **Insider Tip**: Bring a book or a journal—this is the perfect place for quiet contemplation.

2. Wallenstein Garden: Baroque Beauty

Situated near the Charles Bridge, the Wallenstein Garden is a masterpiece of Baroque landscaping. It's part of the Wallenstein Palace, which houses the Czech Senate.

- **Why Visit**: Marvel at ornamental fountains, geometric hedges, and statues inspired by Greek mythology. The garden is also home to a charming artificial grotto and playful koi fish ponds.
- **Insider Tip**: Visit in the early morning or late afternoon to enjoy the garden with fewer visitors.

3. Franciscan Garden: A Green Refuge

Nestled between bustling streets near Wenceslas Square, the Franciscan Garden offers a surprising escape in the city center.

- **Why Visit**: Relax among the neatly arranged flower beds, fragrant rose bushes, and shaded benches. The garden's quiet atmosphere contrasts beautifully with the busy streets just beyond its gates.
- **Insider Tip**: Grab a takeaway coffee from a nearby café and enjoy a peaceful break here.

4. Petrin Hill and the Rose Garden

While Petrin Hill is a well-known attraction, its rose garden remains a tranquil spot that's often overlooked. Located near the Strahov Monastery, this garden is a romantic haven with vibrant blooms and panoramic views.

- **Why Visit**: Stroll through rows of colorful roses, enjoy the scent of fresh flowers, and take in the sweeping views of Prague's rooftops.
- **Insider Tip**: Pair your visit with a climb up the Petrin Lookout Tower for an unforgettable perspective of the city.

5. Gröbovka (Havlíčkovy Sady): A Vineyard Escape

This park, set in the Vršovice district, is home to a picturesque vineyard and a neo-Renaissance villa. It's a perfect blend of natural beauty and historic charm.

- **Why Visit**: Wander the vine-covered slopes, sip local wine at the vineyard café, and soak in the serenity of this lesser-visited park.
- **Insider Tip**: Visit during sunset for breathtaking views of the city bathed in golden light.

6. Vyšehrad Gardens

Set atop the historic Vyšehrad fortress, these gardens are as scenic as they are peaceful. With ancient ruins and panoramic views of the Vltava River, they offer a unique blend of history and tranquility.

- **Why Visit**: Explore the lush greenery, admire the sculptures, and take in the serene atmosphere of this historic site.
- **Insider Tip**: Combine your visit with a walk along the Vyšehrad ramparts for stunning vistas of Prague.

Practical Tips for Visiting Prague's Secret Gardens

- **Timing**: Weekday mornings are typically quieter, giving you the chance to enjoy these spots at your own pace.
- **Respect the Space**: Many of these gardens are local treasures, so keep noise levels down and avoid leaving any litter.
- **Getting There**: Use public transport or enjoy a leisurely walk to discover these hidden green spaces.

Finding Solace in Prague's Green Retreats

Prague's secret gardens and quiet spots provide more than just a break from sightseeing; they offer moments of serenity that stay with you long after you leave. Whether you're drawn to the historic charm of Wallenstein Garden or the romantic beauty of the rose garden on Petrin Hill, these peaceful havens reveal a softer, more intimate side of the city.

Unique Museums and Galleries

Prague's vibrant cultural scene extends beyond its famous landmarks and iconic museums. Tucked away from the usual tourist routes, the city boasts a collection of unique museums and galleries that offer a deeper, often quirky, insight into its history, art, and identity. Whether you're a history buff, art lover, or someone seeking the unconventional, these hidden cultural gems promise a memorable experience.

1. Museum of Alchemists and Magicians of Old Prague

Step into the mysterious world of alchemy and uncover Prague's esoteric past. This intriguing museum, located near Prague Castle, dives into the city's fascination with alchemy during the reign of Emperor Rudolf II.

- **Why Visit**: Explore recreated alchemical laboratories, learn about the mystical practices of the time, and hear tales of magicians who sought to turn base metals into gold.
- **Insider Tip**: The rooftop offers an incredible view of the city, making your visit even more rewarding.

2. Museum Kampa

Situated along the Vltava River, this contemporary art museum is housed in a historic watermill. It focuses on modern art from Central Europe, showcasing works that challenge the boundaries of creativity.

- **Why Visit**: Admire thought-provoking sculptures, installations, and paintings, including pieces by renowned Czech artist František Kupka. The museum's riverside location is an attraction in itself.
- **Insider Tip**: Don't miss the outdoor sculptures, including the iconic crawling babies by artist David Černý.

3. Speculum Alchemiae

Hidden beneath Prague's Old Town lies Speculum Alchemiae, a museum that reveals a network of ancient alchemical laboratories dating back to the

16th century. This underground gem offers a fascinating glimpse into Prague's mystical history.

- **Why Visit**: Wander through the reconstructed labs, learn about ancient alchemical techniques, and see original artifacts. The museum also offers guided tours to enrich your understanding.
- **Insider Tip**: Pair your visit with a walk through the surrounding streets to explore more of Prague's medieval charm.

4. Kafka Museum

Dedicated to Prague's literary legend, Franz Kafka, this museum delves into the life and works of one of the most influential writers of the 20th century. It's an intimate and immersive experience for fans of Kafka's haunting prose.

- **Why Visit**: Browse rare manuscripts, photographs, and letters, while the exhibits transport you into the surreal and melancholic world of Kafka's imagination.
- **Insider Tip**: Look out for the quirky fountain outside the museum, another creation by David Černý.

5. Museum of Miniatures

Prepare to be amazed by tiny masterpieces that require a magnifying glass to truly appreciate. This museum, located within the Strahov Monastery complex, features intricate miniatures that push the limits of human creativity.

- **Why Visit**: Marvel at works like the Lord's Prayer written on a human hair or a camel caravan passing through the eye of a needle. It's a testament to precision and patience.
- **Insider Tip**: Combine your visit with a stop at the Strahov Library for a day of intellectual inspiration.

6. Czech Museum of Music

Set in a former Baroque church, the Czech Museum of Music celebrates the country's rich musical heritage.

It's an auditory and visual journey through centuries of musical history.

- **Why Visit**: Admire a vast collection of instruments, manuscripts, and audio exhibits that highlight the evolution of Czech music. The museum often hosts live performances to complement the experience.
- **Insider Tip**: Check the museum's event schedule for special concerts and workshops.

7. DOX Centre for Contemporary Art

For those who crave cutting-edge creativity, the DOX Centre in Prague's Holešovice district is a must-visit. This gallery blends art, architecture, and ideas to provoke thought and inspire dialogue.

- **Why Visit**: Explore dynamic exhibitions that address current social and political issues. The gallery's unique design, including its iconic airship installation, is an attraction in itself.
- **Insider Tip**: The on-site café is a great spot to relax and discuss the thought-provoking exhibits with fellow visitors.

Practical Tips for Exploring Prague's Unique Museums and Galleries

- **Tickets**: Some museums offer discounted admission on certain days or for students and seniors, so it's worth checking in advance.
- **Timing**: Arrive early to avoid crowds, especially at smaller venues where space may be limited.
- **Combine Visits**: Plan your day to include nearby attractions or dining spots for a more seamless experience.

Discovering Prague's Unconventional Side

Prague's unique museums and galleries provide a refreshing contrast to the city's traditional sights. They offer visitors a chance to delve deeper into the city's soul, uncovering stories and perspectives that are often overlooked. Whether it's the mystical world of alchemy or the avant-garde creations of contemporary artists, these cultural experiences promise to leave a lasting impression on your journey.

Chapter Eight

A Foodie's Guide to Prague

Traditional Czech Dishes You Must Try

One of the most rewarding aspects of visiting Prague is indulging in its traditional cuisine. Czech food is a celebration of hearty, comforting flavors that reflect the country's agricultural roots and its rich cultural heritage. Whether you're dining at a high-end restaurant or a cozy local tavern, you'll find dishes that showcase the best of Czech culinary traditions. Here's what to add to your must-try list:

1. Svíčková na Smetaně (Marinated Beef with Cream Sauce)

This beloved dish is a staple of Czech dining. Tender slices of marinated beef are served in a creamy vegetable-based sauce, typically made with root vegetables, cream, and a touch of lemon. It's usually accompanied by bread dumplings, a hallmark of Czech cuisine.

- **Why Try It**: The combination of rich flavors and textures makes it an unforgettable experience.

- **Insider Tip**: Pair it with a Czech pilsner for a true local experience.

2. Vepřo Knedlo Zelo (Pork, Dumplings, and Sauerkraut)

Often referred to as the national dish of the Czech Republic, this hearty plate features roasted pork served with fluffy bread dumplings and tangy sauerkraut. It's simple yet deeply satisfying.

- **Why Try It**: It's the ultimate comfort food and a great way to immerse yourself in Czech tradition.
- **Insider Tip**: Look for restaurants offering homemade dumplings for an authentic touch.

3. Trdelník (Chimney Cake)

Though its origins are debated, trdelník has become a must-have treat in Prague. This sweet pastry is made by wrapping dough around a spit, roasting it over an open flame, and coating it with sugar, cinnamon, and nuts. Many stalls also fill it with ice cream or Nutella for a modern twist.

- **Why Try It**: It's a fun street food experience and perfect for a quick snack while exploring the city.
- **Insider Tip**: Visit smaller bakeries instead of tourist-heavy stalls for better quality.

4. Kulajda (Dill Soup)

This creamy soup combines potatoes, mushrooms, dill, and a touch of vinegar for a tangy, aromatic flavor. It's often topped with a poached egg for added richness.

- **Why Try It**: It's a warm, comforting dish that's perfect for chilly days in Prague.
- **Insider Tip**: Some upscale restaurants add modern twists like truffle oil or smoked bacon.

5. Bramboráky (Potato Pancakes)

Crispy and flavorful, these potato pancakes are seasoned with garlic, marjoram, and spices. They can be served as a side dish or enjoyed on their own, sometimes with a dollop of sour cream.

- **Why Try It**: They're an excellent example of Czech street food and a perfect option for vegetarians.
- **Insider Tip**: Try them fresh from the pan for the best texture and flavor.

6. Tatarák (Czech Steak Tartare)

A favorite among locals, tatarák is finely chopped raw beef seasoned with onions, spices, and sometimes a splash of beer. It's typically served with toasted bread rubbed with garlic.

- **Why Try It**: For adventurous eaters, this dish offers a unique insight into Czech culinary preferences.
- **Insider Tip**: Always order it at reputable restaurants to ensure top-quality ingredients.

7. Czech Desserts: Buchty and Koláče

For those with a sweet tooth, Czech pastries are a must. Buchty are soft yeast buns filled with fruit or poppy seeds, while koláče are round pastries with sweet fillings like plum jam, cottage cheese, or poppy seeds.

- **Why Try Them**: These traditional baked goods highlight the Czech love for homemade treats.
- **Insider Tip**: Visit local bakeries early in the morning to enjoy them fresh out of the oven.

Practical Tips for Enjoying Czech Cuisine

- **Local Taverns**: For the most authentic experience, eat at local pubs or "hospody." They often serve generous portions at reasonable prices.
- **Portion Sizes**: Czech dishes tend to be filling, so pace yourself, especially if you're planning to sample multiple items.
- **Dietary Needs**: While traditional cuisine leans heavily on meat and dairy, many restaurants now offer vegetarian or gluten-free adaptations.

Prague's culinary landscape is as rich and diverse as its history, offering visitors a delicious way to connect with the culture. By exploring these traditional dishes, you'll take home not just memories, but also a deeper appreciation for Czech heritage.

Best Restaurants and Cafés

Prague's food scene is a delightful mix of tradition and innovation. From historic restaurants serving time-honored Czech classics to contemporary cafés offering artisanal coffee and globally inspired dishes, the city caters to every palate. Here's a curated guide to some of Prague's best dining spots to help you savor its culinary essence.

Fine Dining Experiences

If you're looking to indulge in an elevated culinary journey, Prague has a growing number of fine dining establishments that artfully blend Czech traditions with modern gastronomy.

- **La Degustation Bohême Bourgeoise**: This Michelin-starred restaurant is a celebration of Czech flavors with a contemporary twist. Each dish is meticulously crafted using seasonal and local ingredients. Opt for the tasting menu to fully experience its culinary creativity.

- *Insider Tip*: Reserve a table well in advance, as it's one of the most sought-after dining experiences in Prague.
- **Field Restaurant**: Another Michelin-starred gem, Field focuses on Nordic-inspired cuisine with an emphasis on foraged and organic ingredients. Its minimalist approach lets the flavors truly shine.
  - *Why Visit*: The presentation is a feast for the eyes, and the flavors are unforgettable.

Traditional Czech Restaurants

For a more authentic and hearty experience, head to one of Prague's traditional eateries.

- **Lokál**: A chain of taverns offering simple yet expertly prepared Czech dishes like *svíčková* and *vepřo knedlo zelo*. Their beer is always fresh, as it's tapped straight from the tank.
  - *What to Try*: The fried cheese with tartar sauce is a favorite among locals and visitors alike.
- **U Modré Kachničky (The Blue Duckling)**: Step into a fairytale setting and enjoy Czech specialties such as roasted duck or wild game dishes. The cozy, old-world charm adds to the experience.

- ○ *Why Visit*: Perfect for a romantic dinner or a special occasion.

Casual and Cozy Cafés

Prague's café culture is a reflection of its literary and artistic past, with many establishments offering a charming atmosphere to enjoy coffee, pastries, and light meals.

- **Café Louvre**: This historic café, once frequented by Franz Kafka and Albert Einstein, exudes an old-world elegance. It's an excellent spot for coffee, breakfast, or a light lunch.
  - ○ *What to Try*: The creamy hot chocolate and apple strudel are local favorites.

- **Můj Šálek Kávy**: Known for its exceptional coffee and relaxed vibe, this modern café in the Karlín district is a must-visit for coffee enthusiasts.
  - *Insider Tip*: Arrive early on weekends to snag a table—it's a popular brunch spot.
- **Café Slavia**: Overlooking the Vltava River, this iconic café has been a gathering place for intellectuals and artists for decades. Its grand interiors and scenic views make it a timeless choice.
  - *What to Try*: Pair your espresso with a slice of honey cake.

Global Flavors in Prague

While traditional Czech cuisine takes center stage, Prague's international dining scene is thriving.

- **Eska**: Located in Karlín, this innovative restaurant merges Czech traditions with global influences. The open kitchen adds a lively touch to your dining experience.
  - *Why Visit*: Their house-made sourdough bread and fermented dishes are a highlight.
- **Sansho**: For an Asian-inspired menu with Czech ingredients, Sansho is a game-changer. Their slow-cooked pork belly and soft-shell crab are crowd favorites.

- *Insider Tip*: Go for the tasting menu to sample the chef's best creations.

Budget-Friendly Eats

Prague also offers plenty of affordable yet satisfying options for those traveling on a budget.

- **Havelská Koruna**: This self-service restaurant in the Old Town is ideal for trying Czech classics without breaking the bank.
  - *What to Try*: Their *goulash* is a hearty and flavorful option.
- **Bageterie Boulevard**: A popular local chain offering fresh sandwiches, salads, and soups. Perfect for a quick, affordable bite.

Sweet Stops and Dessert Havens

No trip to Prague is complete without indulging your sweet tooth.

- **Crème de la Crème**: This gelato shop is a local favorite, offering unique flavors like poppy seed and mulled wine.
  - *Why Visit*: It's a refreshing treat after a day of exploring the city.
- **Pekárna Praktika**: A bakery that prides itself on using organic ingredients and traditional baking methods. Their pastries and sourdough loaves are exceptional.

Practical Tips for Dining in Prague

- **Reservations**: Popular restaurants, especially fine dining spots, often require advance reservations.
- **Tipping**: A tip of 10-15% is customary if the service is satisfactory.
- **Peak Hours**: Many restaurants fill up quickly during lunch and dinner hours, so plan accordingly.

From luxurious feasts to casual bites, Prague's dining options cater to every mood and budget. Exploring its restaurants and cafés is not just about the food—it's about experiencing the city's heart and soul through its culinary traditions.

Vegan and Vegetarian Options

Prague's culinary landscape has blossomed in recent years to accommodate a growing demand for vegan and vegetarian dining. Whether you're a dedicated herbivore or simply exploring plant-based options, the city offers an array of restaurants, cafés, and markets that cater to your preferences. From traditional Czech recipes with a modern twist to globally inspired dishes, Prague is a welcoming destination for meat-free dining.

Plant-Based Czech Cuisine

Czech food is traditionally meat-heavy, but many restaurants are reimagining classic dishes to suit vegan and vegetarian diets.

- **Lehká Hlava (Clear Head)**: A cozy, atmospheric vegetarian restaurant offering creative interpretations of Czech and international dishes.
    - *What to Try*: Their vegan *svíčková*, a reimagined version of the Czech creamy vegetable sauce, is both hearty and satisfying.
- **Etnosvět**: Known for its elegant and globally inspired menu, Etnosvět offers a vegetarian dining experience that feels upscale.
    - *Why Visit*: The tasting menu allows you to explore a variety of flavors, and the plating is Instagram-worthy.

Vegan-Only Restaurants

Prague boasts a vibrant vegan scene, with many restaurants dedicated solely to plant-based cuisine.

- **Vegan's Prague**: Located near Prague Castle, this restaurant serves vegan takes on Czech classics and international dishes.

- ○ *What to Try*: The vegan *svíčková* or the tempeh burger paired with their homemade lemonade.
  - ○ *Insider Tip*: The rooftop terrace offers stunning views of the city, perfect for a leisurely meal.
- **Plevel**: A rustic eatery with a focus on fresh, locally sourced ingredients. Their menu rotates seasonally but always features innovative vegan options.
  - ○ *Why Visit*: The earthy atmosphere and friendly service make it feel like home.

International Flavors

For those craving something beyond Czech cuisine, Prague's international vegan and vegetarian offerings are sure to impress.

- **Loving Hut**: This global vegan chain has multiple locations in Prague, serving an extensive menu of Asian-inspired dishes.
  - ○ *What to Try*: Their vegan pho and crispy tofu dishes are crowd-pleasers.
- **Chutnej**: A vegan bistro specializing in vibrant bowls, burgers, and smoothies. Perfect for a quick yet satisfying meal.
  - ○ *Why Visit*: The portions are generous, and the flavors are bold.

Cafés with Vegan-Friendly Menus

Prague's café culture extends its warm embrace to vegan and vegetarian visitors, with many spots offering plant-based options.

- **Moment Café**: A popular hangout spot for vegan breakfast and brunch.
    - ○ *What to Try*: Their tofu scramble or vegan pancakes paired with oat milk lattes.
- **MyRaw Café**: A haven for raw food enthusiasts, offering everything from smoothies to raw vegan cakes.
    - ○ *Insider Tip*: Their raw vegan tiramisu is a must-try.

Markets and Grocery Stores

For self-caterers or those seeking vegan snacks, Prague's markets and stores provide plenty of options.

- **Náměstí Republiky Farmers' Market**: This market often features stalls with vegan baked goods, fresh produce, and locally made products.
  - ○ *Insider Tip*: Visit early to grab the freshest items and avoid crowds.
- **BioPoint**: A chain of organic and health food stores stocked with plant-based staples, from vegan cheese to gluten-free bread.

Practical Tips for Vegan and Vegetarian Dining in Prague

- **Language Help**: Learn a few key phrases, like "jsem vegan" (I am vegan) or "jsem vegetarián" (I am vegetarian), to help communicate your dietary needs.
- **Menus**: Many restaurants mark vegan and vegetarian options with symbols, making it easier to identify suitable dishes.
- **Reservations**: Popular vegan restaurants like Vegan's Prague can fill up quickly, so it's best to book in advance.

With its expanding array of plant-based options, Prague is an increasingly vegan- and vegetarian-friendly destination. The city's chefs have embraced the challenge of creating flavorful and innovative dishes, ensuring you'll leave with not just a full stomach but a deeper appreciation for Prague's culinary creativity.

Prague's Craft Beer Scene

Prague isn't just the birthplace of pilsner; it's also become a haven for craft beer enthusiasts. With a long-standing brewing tradition dating back centuries, the Czech Republic is synonymous with beer. Yet, in recent years, the craft beer movement has exploded, and the city has evolved into a dynamic hub for unique, small-batch brews. Whether you're a connoisseur or simply curious about the local beer culture, Prague offers an abundance of breweries, bars, and festivals to explore.

A Rich History of Czech Beer

Before we dive into the modern-day craft scene, it's worth noting that beer has always been central to Czech culture. The country has one of the highest beer consumption rates in the world, and brewing traditions run deep. Prague's beer culture isn't just about drinking; it's about celebrating the art of brewing passed down through generations.

The Czech pilsner, created in the 19th century in Plzeň, revolutionized beer globally, and you'll find it everywhere in Prague. But, beyond pilsner, Czech brewers also specialize in darker beers like *tmavé* (dark lager) and *světlé* (light lager), as well as unique regional styles. However, in recent years, the craft beer movement has infused Prague with new energy, and local brewers have embraced experimental styles, pushing the boundaries of Czech brewing.

Where to Find Craft Beer in Prague

While large breweries like Pilsner Urquell dominate, it's the smaller, independent microbreweries and craft beer pubs that are giving Prague's beer scene its contemporary flair.

- **BeerGeek Bar**: A paradise for craft beer lovers, BeerGeek boasts an impressive selection of local and international craft brews. With dozens of taps pouring a wide range of styles, this cozy bar offers something for every taste, from rich stouts to tangy sours.
    - *What to Try*: The rotating selection of seasonal brews is always a highlight. Ask the staff for recommendations based on your preferences.
- **The Craft Beer Museum**: Located in the heart of Old Town, this museum offers a fascinating introduction to the world of Czech beer, alongside a lively bar serving craft beer from some of the city's best microbreweries. It's an excellent starting point for understanding the local beer culture.

- *What to Try*: Sample a flight of beers from different Prague-based breweries to get a taste of the city's variety.
- **Pivovarský Dům**: An iconic Prague brewpub that brews its own beer on-site. Known for its cozy atmosphere and delicious Czech fare paired with freshly brewed beer, it's a great spot to experience the essence of Czech brewing.
  - *What to Try*: Their *razené pivo* (smoked beer) and house-brewed *pilsner* are unique to the brewery and showcase local flavors.

Local Microbreweries to Explore

Prague is home to a growing number of craft breweries, each with its own distinct style and offerings. These small, independent brewers take pride in their ability to experiment with flavors and techniques that make Prague's beer scene stand out from the more mainstream options.

- **Malesov Brewery**: Located just outside the city, Malesov is known for producing innovative ales and lagers with a distinct Czech touch. Their beers are brewed with locally sourced ingredients and are celebrated for their balance of tradition and experimentation.
  - *What to Try*: Their *IPA* (India Pale Ale) offers a bold twist on the traditional Czech beer palate.
- **Czech Craft Beer Festival**: Every year, Prague hosts the Czech Craft Beer Festival, a must-visit event for beer lovers. This festival gathers dozens of local breweries under one roof, offering an unparalleled opportunity to taste unique brews from across the country.
  - *Insider Tip*: Plan ahead to attend this festival if you're visiting during the spring or summer. It's an experience that lets you taste the creativity of Czech brewing.

Craft Beer Trends in Prague

The craft beer scene in Prague is dynamic and ever-evolving. Breweries are increasingly experimenting with flavors, styles, and techniques from across the globe. While the Czech tradition of lager brewing remains strong, there's a noticeable rise in demand for hops-forward beers like IPAs, barrel-aged brews, and even fruit-infused beers. If you're a fan of sour beers, you'll find some exceptional options from Prague's craft breweries.

The local brewing community is also highly collaborative. Many craft brewers team up to create limited-edition brews or share their brewing knowledge. This sense of camaraderie among local breweries gives Prague's craft beer scene an intimate, community-driven feel.

Practical Tips for Enjoying Prague's Craft Beer Scene

- **Czech Beer Etiquette**: When ordering beer in Prague, it's customary to ask for a *malý* (small) or *velký* (large) pint. Also, if you're at a traditional beer hall, don't be surprised if the bartender offers you a *polotmavé* or *tmavé* beer instead of a lager; it's a popular choice for locals.

- **Tasting Flights**: Many craft beer bars and breweries offer tasting flights, so take advantage of this option to sample a variety of styles and find your favorite.

- **Beer and Food Pairing**: Czech food pairs beautifully with beer. Don't miss the chance to enjoy some hearty *schnitzel*, rich *svíčková*, or savory *goulash* alongside your craft beer.

Prague's craft beer scene is a delightful mix of innovation, tradition, and experimentation. Whether you're visiting one of the city's iconic craft beer pubs, exploring a microbrewery, or attending a beer festival, you'll find that Prague offers a truly immersive experience for beer enthusiasts.

Chapter Nine

Experiencing Prague by Day and Night

Daytime Adventures: Parks, Markets, and More

Prague is a city that brims with life from sunrise to sunset, offering an array of experiences for every type of traveler. Whether you're looking to unwind in lush green spaces, hunt for treasures at vibrant markets, or delve into the city's history, Prague's daytime activities promise memorable adventures. Here's a detailed look at how to make the most of your days in this magical city.

Strolling Through Prague's Beautiful Parks

Prague's parks and gardens are perfect for those seeking a break from the hustle and bustle of the city center. These green oases not only provide a chance to relax but also offer stunning views and historical intrigue.

- **Letná Park**: Perched on a hill overlooking the Vltava River, Letná Park is a favorite among locals and tourists alike. With sprawling lawns, tree-lined paths, and one of the best panoramic views of Prague's bridges, it's an ideal spot for a leisurely stroll or a picnic. Don't forget to visit the massive metronome sculpture, a modern art installation that has become a symbol of the park.

- ○ *Insider Tip*: Stop by one of the park's beer gardens for a refreshing drink with a view.
- **Petřín Hill and Gardens**: For a more immersive experience, head to Petřín Hill. This expansive park is home to the Petřín Lookout Tower, often called Prague's "mini Eiffel Tower." You can climb the tower for breathtaking views or wander through the beautiful rose gardens and orchards.
  - ○ *Insider Tip*: The funicular railway is a fun way to reach the top of the hill, especially if you're traveling with kids.
- **Stromovka Park**: Known as Prague's "Central Park," Stromovka is a serene retreat ideal for jogging, cycling, or simply lounging by the ponds. Once a royal game reserve, this park offers a quieter escape compared to the more popular spots.

Exploring Prague's Markets

Markets are the heart of Prague's daytime charm, offering a glimpse into local life and culture. Whether you're in the mood for fresh produce, handmade crafts, or unique souvenirs, Prague's markets have it all.

- **Havelská Market**: Located in the Old Town, this historic market dates back to the 13th century and is one of Prague's oldest. You'll find stalls selling everything from fresh fruits and vegetables to traditional Czech wooden toys and souvenirs.
  - *What to Buy*: Look for hand-painted ceramic items and marionettes, two quintessential Czech crafts.
- **Náplavka Farmers' Market**: Situated along the Vltava River, this bustling market is a weekend highlight. It's a favorite spot for locals to shop for organic produce, artisanal bread, and freshly brewed coffee. The lively atmosphere, with live music and food trucks, makes it an experience to savor.
  - *Insider Tip*: Arrive early to beat the crowds and enjoy breakfast by the river.
- **Kolbenova Flea Market**: For those who love hunting for vintage treasures, Kolbenova is the place to be. This sprawling market on the outskirts of Prague is a treasure trove of antiques, collectibles, and quirky finds.
  - *Insider Tip*: Bring cash, as many vendors don't accept cards, and be ready to haggle for the best deals.

Daytime Cultural Activities

If you're a culture enthusiast, Prague's daytime offerings extend well beyond its landmarks. The city hosts various exhibitions, workshops, and performances that provide deeper insights into its vibrant traditions.

- **DOX Centre for Contemporary Art**: Step into Prague's contemporary art scene at DOX, a cutting-edge gallery showcasing thought-provoking exhibitions and innovative installations. It's a refreshing contrast to the city's historical art and architecture.
- **Municipal House**: This Art Nouveau masterpiece is not just a concert venue but also

a hub of cultural activity. Guided tours provide a behind-the-scenes look at its opulent interiors, while the café and restaurant are perfect for a mid-day treat.

- **National Technical Museum**: A great option for families, this museum showcases Prague's contributions to science and technology. From vintage automobiles to historic aviation exhibits, there's something to fascinate visitors of all ages.

Tips for Enjoying Prague by Day

1. **Start Early**: Prague's main attractions and parks can get busy, especially during peak seasons. Arriving early ensures a more serene experience and the chance to capture stunning photos.
2. **Wear Comfortable Shoes**: With its cobblestone streets and hilly parks, comfortable footwear is essential for exploring Prague.
3. **Plan for Snacks**: Prague's parks and markets are dotted with vendors selling delicious treats. Indulge in a traditional *trdelník* (chimney cake) or grab a freshly baked pastry to enjoy on the go.
4. **Stay Hydrated**: While exploring, keep a bottle of water handy, especially during the warmer months.

Prague's daytime adventures offer a delightful mix of relaxation, exploration, and cultural immersion. Whether you're soaking in the views from a hilltop park, savoring local flavors at a vibrant market, or diving into the city's contemporary art scene, you'll find that Prague truly comes alive in the daylight.

Prague After Dark: Bars, Nightclubs, and Cultural Performances

When the sun dips below Prague's skyline, the city transforms into a vibrant hub of nightlife and culture. Whether you're seeking lively bars, pulsating nightclubs, or a more refined evening of theater and music, Prague's nocturnal offerings cater to all tastes. Here's how to make the most of your evenings in this magical city.

Bars and Pubs: Where History Meets Creativity

Prague is a city where you can sip a craft cocktail in a sleek, modern bar one night and enjoy a pint of beer in a centuries-old pub the next. The bar scene here is diverse, blending tradition and innovation.

- **Hemingway Bar**: For cocktail enthusiasts, Hemingway Bar is a must-visit. This intimate venue, inspired by the legendary writer Ernest Hemingway, offers a sophisticated atmosphere and an impressive menu of expertly crafted drinks.
    - *Insider Tip*: Try their signature absinthe-based cocktails for a taste of

Prague's bohemian past, but be sure to book a table in advance, as it's a popular spot.

- **Beer Halls and Traditional Pubs**: Prague is synonymous with beer, and its beer halls and pubs are cultural institutions.
  - *U Fleků*: One of Prague's oldest breweries, U Fleků has been serving beer since 1499. Pair your pint with hearty Czech dishes while enjoying live accordion music.
  - *Lokál*: Known for its fresh, unpasteurized Pilsner, Lokál is a great place for a casual drink in a relaxed setting.
- **Letná Beer Gardens**: For a more laid-back experience, head to one of Prague's beer gardens, such as those in Letná Park or Riegrovy Sady. They're perfect for unwinding with a cold drink and enjoying the city's twinkling lights.

Nightclubs: Dance the Night Away

Prague's clubbing scene is as dynamic as its history, offering everything from underground techno to high-energy dance floors.

- **Karlovy Lazne**: Known as the largest nightclub in Central Europe, Karlovy Lazne boasts five floors, each with a different music genre. Whether you're into electronic beats, old-school disco, or R&B, there's something for everyone here.
  - *Insider Tip*: Go early to avoid long queues and explore each floor before the crowds arrive.
- **Roxy**: A favorite among locals and tourists alike, Roxy is one of Prague's premier clubs. With a focus on electronic music and live performances, it's a go-to spot for a memorable night out.
- **Cross Club**: This unique venue in Holešovice is a blend of nightclub and art installation. Its

steampunk-inspired décor, coupled with eclectic music ranging from dubstep to reggae, makes it a standout experience.

Cultural Performances: A Refined Evening

If loud music and crowded dance floors aren't your style, Prague's cultural offerings provide a more sophisticated way to spend your evenings.

- **Classical Music and Opera**: Prague's rich musical heritage is alive and well, with performances held in stunning venues.
  - *Rudolfinum*: Home to the Czech Philharmonic Orchestra, this grand concert hall hosts a variety of classical music performances.

- *State Opera*: Experience the magic of opera in this opulent venue, which showcases both traditional and modern productions.
- **Black Light Theater**: A uniquely Prague experience, black light theater combines mime, dance, and ultraviolet lighting to create mesmerizing performances. The shows are largely visual, making them accessible even if you don't speak Czech.
  - *Insider Tip*: Check out Theater Ta Fantastika, one of the city's best-known black light theaters.
- **Jazz Clubs**: For a relaxed yet lively evening, Prague's jazz clubs are the perfect choice.
  - *Jazz Dock*: Situated on the river, this modern venue offers an intimate setting for live jazz performances.
  - *Reduta Jazz Club*: A historic jazz spot where legends like Bill Clinton have played, Reduta is a must-visit for music lovers.

Nighttime Tips for a Safe and Enjoyable Experience

1. **Plan Your Transportation**: Prague's public transportation runs late, but it's a good idea to familiarize yourself with night tram and bus schedules. Taxis and rideshare services like Bolt and Uber are reliable options for getting around after dark.

2. **Stay Alert**: Like any major city, Prague's nightlife areas can get busy, so keep an eye on your belongings, especially in crowded venues.

3. **Dress the Part**: While most bars and pubs have a casual dress code, some upscale bars and clubs may require smart attire.

4. **Stay Hydrated and Snack Smart**: Between drinks, remember to hydrate and sample some of Prague's late-night snacks, like a freshly grilled sausage from a street vendor.

Prague's nightlife offers a captivating mix of energy and elegance. Whether you're raising a glass at a historic pub, dancing to the beats of an underground DJ, or soaking in the melodies of a classical symphony, your evenings in Prague are bound to be as unforgettable as its picturesque days.

Chapter Ten

Shopping in Prague

Souvenirs Worth Taking Home

Shopping for souvenirs in Prague is an opportunity to take a piece of its charm back home with you. The city offers a treasure trove of items that reflect its rich history, craftsmanship, and cultural traditions. Whether you're searching for a meaningful keepsake or a unique gift, Prague's offerings ensure you'll find something special.

Bohemian Crystal: Timeless Elegance

Bohemian crystal is one of the most iconic souvenirs from Prague. Known for its exquisite craftsmanship and intricate designs, it has been a symbol of Czech artistry for centuries.

- **What to Look For**: Vases, glasses, chandeliers, and jewelry are among the most popular items. Many pieces feature traditional hand-cut patterns or vibrant colors.
- **Where to Buy**: Visit shops like **Moser** or **Preciosa** for premium-quality crystal. For more affordable options, check out smaller shops around the Old Town.

- *Insider Tip*: Ensure you're buying authentic Bohemian crystal by asking for a certificate of authenticity.

Czech Garnet: A Sparkling Memento

Czech garnet, a deep-red gemstone mined locally, is a coveted souvenir that holds both beauty and history. It's often set in silver or gold jewelry and makes for a striking gift or personal keepsake.

- **What to Look For**: Rings, necklaces, earrings, and brooches featuring garnet stones.
- **Where to Buy**: Opt for trusted retailers like **Granát Turnov**, a cooperative dedicated to producing genuine Czech garnet jewelry.
- *Insider Tip*: Beware of imitations and shop only at reputable stores to ensure you're getting authentic stones.

Marionettes and Puppets: A Touch of Whimsy

Marionettes and puppets are deeply ingrained in Czech culture, making them a unique and playful souvenir. These handcrafted items range from traditional designs to modern characters.

- **What to Look For**: Hand-carved wooden puppets or elaborately dressed marionettes.

- **Where to Buy**: Check out **Truhlář Marionety** or the shops near Charles Bridge for high-quality, artisan-made pieces.
- *Insider Tip*: Some shops allow you to see the puppets in action or even commission a custom design.

Beer and Glassware: A Taste of Prague

Czechia is synonymous with beer, and bringing home a bottle or two of local brews is a must for any beer enthusiast. Pair it with traditional Czech beer mugs or glasses for an authentic experience.

- **What to Look For**: Pilsner Urquell, Budweiser Budvar, or unique craft brews from Prague's microbreweries.

- **Where to Buy**: Larger supermarkets like **Tesco** or specialty beer shops like **BeerGeek** offer a wide selection.
- *Insider Tip*: Many breweries sell exclusive editions or gift sets that make for perfect souvenirs.

Traditional Czech Toys: Nostalgia and Charm

Wooden toys are a delightful nod to Czech traditions, blending practicality with charm. These make excellent gifts for children or nostalgic adults.

- **What to Look For**: Wooden puzzles, pull-along animals, or building sets like the Czech-made **Merkur** construction kit.
- **Where to Buy**: Look for shops like **Hračky U Zlatého Lva** (Toys at the Golden Lion) in Old Town.

Absinthe and Becherovka: Local Spirits

If you're looking for a more spirited souvenir, Czechia's famous absinthe and the herbal liqueur Becherovka are excellent choices.

- **What to Look For**: Bottles of green absinthe, traditionally enjoyed with sugar and water, or the cinnamon and clove-infused Becherovka.
- **Where to Buy**: Specialty liquor stores or larger markets carry these iconic beverages.

- *Insider Tip*: Opt for smaller, artisanal brands for a unique twist on these classic spirits.

Handmade Ceramics and Porcelain

Czech ceramics and porcelain reflect the country's artistry and attention to detail. These items are both practical and decorative.

- **What to Look For**: Teapots, plates, and mugs featuring traditional Czech patterns or modern designs.
- **Where to Buy**: Stores like **Blue and White** specialize in handmade porcelain.

Books and Posters: A Literary Keepsake

For a more personal and literary souvenir, consider a book by a famous Czech author like Franz Kafka or a vintage-style poster showcasing Prague's landmarks.

- **What to Look For**: English translations of Kafka's works, or art nouveau posters inspired by Alphonse Mucha.
- **Where to Buy**: Visit **Kafka Bookstore** or poster shops near Wenceslas Square.

Tips for Shopping Souvenirs in Prague

1. **Bargain Wisely**: While many shops have fixed prices, haggling is acceptable in markets. Be polite and respectful when negotiating.
2. **Check for Authenticity**: Especially for high-value items like crystal and garnet, always ask for a certificate of authenticity.

3. **Pack Carefully**: Fragile items like crystal or ceramics require extra care. Consider investing in travel-safe packaging or shipping options.

Local Markets and Boutiques

Shopping in Prague offers a delightful mix of bustling markets and charming boutiques, each brimming with unique finds that reflect the city's culture and craftsmanship. Exploring these vibrant spaces is an experience in itself, allowing you to connect with local artisans and discover one-of-a-kind treasures.

Farmers' Markets: Fresh Finds and Local Flavors

Farmers' markets in Prague are more than just places to shop—they're a celebration of Czech produce, handmade goods, and a sense of community.

- **What to Expect**: Fresh fruits, vegetables, artisanal cheeses, baked goods, and regional specialties. Some markets also feature handmade crafts, flowers, and street food stalls.
- **Top Picks**:
  - **Náplavka Farmers' Market**: Located along the Vltava River, this lively market is a weekend favorite for its scenic setting and diverse offerings. Don't miss the freshly baked pastries and local honey.
  - **Jiřák Farmers' Market**: Situated in the Vinohrady district, this market is smaller but equally charming, known for its organic produce and friendly vendors.
- *Insider Tip*: Arrive early to beat the crowds and snag the freshest items. Bring cash, as some vendors may not accept cards.

Flea Markets: Hunting for Hidden Gems

If you're a fan of vintage finds and quirky treasures, Prague's flea markets are a must-visit. They offer everything from antiques and collectibles to secondhand books and retro fashion.

- **Top Picks**:
  - **Kolbenova Flea Market**: One of the largest in the city, this market is a treasure trove for antique lovers and bargain hunters.
  - **Tylovo náměstí Market**: Though smaller, this market in the New Town offers an eclectic mix of vintage items and handmade crafts.
- *Insider Tip*: Haggling is common at flea markets, so don't hesitate to negotiate for a better deal.

Specialty Boutiques: Unique Artisanal Finds

Prague's boutique scene is a haven for those seeking high-quality, handcrafted items. From fashion and jewelry to home décor and artwork, these shops showcase the creativity of local designers and artisans.

- **Top Picks**:
  - **Artěl**: This boutique specializes in contemporary Czech glassware with modern designs that make for sophisticated souvenirs.

- ○ **Havel's Boutique**: Nestled near Old Town Square, this shop features traditional Czech embroidery, lace, and handmade ceramics.
- ○ **Debut Gallery**: Perfect for art enthusiasts, this boutique-gallery hybrid offers unique pieces by emerging Czech artists.
- *Insider Tip*: Many boutiques in Prague are independently owned, so shopping here directly supports local businesses.

Christmas Markets: A Seasonal Delight

If you're visiting Prague during the winter holidays, the city's Christmas markets are a magical experience.

These markets combine festive décor, seasonal treats, and an array of handcrafted goods.

- **Highlights**: The markets at **Old Town Square** and **Wenceslas Square** are the most popular, offering ornaments, wooden toys, candles, and traditional Czech treats like trdelník (chimney cake).
- *Insider Tip*: Sip on some warm mulled wine (svařák) as you explore, and visit in the evening to enjoy the markets illuminated by twinkling lights.

Local Design Stores: Modern Czech Creativity

For a contemporary twist, Prague's design stores showcase innovative works by modern Czech designers.

- **Top Picks**:
  - **Bohemia Design Market**: A hub for fashion, accessories, and home décor crafted by local talents.
  - **Loom**: Known for its minimalist aesthetic, this shop offers beautiful textiles, ceramics, and paper goods.
- *Insider Tip*: Keep an eye out for limited-edition items, as many of these stores carry small-batch or one-of-a-kind pieces.

Tips for Exploring Markets and Boutiques

1. **Time Your Visit**: Farmers' markets are typically open on weekends, while flea markets often operate on specific days. Plan accordingly.
2. **Cash is King**: While some vendors accept cards, having cash on hand (preferably Czech koruna) will make transactions smoother.
3. **Bring Your Own Bag**: Many markets are eco-conscious and encourage reusable bags.
4. **Be Curious**: Don't hesitate to ask vendors about their products. Many love sharing the stories behind their creations..

High-End Shopping Streets

For those who enjoy luxury shopping, Prague offers a range of upscale streets where global fashion brands meet bespoke Czech design. Strolling through these areas is as much about the experience as it is about the purchases, with grand architecture and polished storefronts adding to the allure.

Pařížská Street: Prague's Luxury Mecca

Located in the heart of the Jewish Quarter, Pařížská Street is synonymous with high-end fashion and elegance. Flanked by art nouveau buildings and tree-lined walkways, this street rivals the world's most famous shopping districts.

- **What You'll Find**: Iconic luxury brands such as Louis Vuitton, Gucci, Prada, and Dior sit alongside Czech fine jewelry houses like Halada and ALO Diamonds.
- **Insider Tip**: Even if you're not planning to shop, Pařížská is worth a visit for window shopping and soaking in the atmosphere. Pair

your stroll with a visit to nearby synagogues or the Old-New Synagogue for a cultural touch.

Na Příkopě: A Blend of Glamour and Accessibility

Na Příkopě is one of Prague's busiest shopping streets, offering a mix of high-end stores and premium department stores. Stretching between Wenceslas Square and Republic Square, it's perfect for those looking to combine luxury shopping with convenience.

- **What You'll Find**: Expect to see brands like Hugo Boss, Michael Kors, and Armani Exchange, along with the renowned Czech glass company, Moser. Nearby department stores like Palladium also house premium brands.
- **Insider Tip**: Visit the Slovanský dům shopping arcade, a hidden gem on this street. It features chic boutiques, fine dining options, and a tranquil garden.

Luxury Shopping Arcades

Prague boasts a number of elegant shopping arcades that provide an exclusive experience in a more intimate setting.

- **Worth Exploring**:

- ○ **Černá Růže**: Located near Na Příkopě, this stylish arcade features boutique stores offering high-quality fashion, jewelry, and accessories.
- ○ **Slovanský dům**: As mentioned above, this arcade is a haven for luxury goods and gourmet restaurants, all set within a beautifully restored historical building.
- **Insider Tip**: These arcades often host exclusive pop-up events and exhibitions. Check their websites or inquire with staff for the latest happenings.

Specialty Stores on Lesser-Known Streets

While Pařížská and Na Příkopě are the stars, some quieter streets also offer upscale shopping opportunities.

- **Dlouhá Street**: Known for its trendy vibe, this street combines modern boutiques with high-end shops. It's a great spot for those seeking bespoke Czech designs alongside global names.
- **Karoliny Světlé Street**: This charming street near the Vltava River offers refined stores specializing in antiques and Czech-made luxury items like leather goods and custom jewelry.

Shopping Tips for High-End Streets

1. **Timing Matters**: Stores generally open around 10 a.m. and close by 7 p.m. Luxury stores often have a more relaxed pace, so don't rush your visit.
2. **Tax-Free Shopping**: As a non-EU visitor, you can claim VAT refunds on purchases over a certain amount. Ask for a tax-free form at participating stores.
3. **Personalized Service**: Many high-end stores offer tailored services such as private fittings or gift wrapping. Don't hesitate to inquire.
4. **Explore Beyond Shopping**: Combine your shopping spree with nearby cultural landmarks for a well-rounded experience.

Shopping on Prague's high-end streets isn't just about acquiring luxury goods; it's about indulging in the city's elegant charm and refined lifestyle. From designer labels on Pařížská to bespoke Czech craftsmanship in boutique arcades, these streets offer a sophisticated side of Prague that's worth exploring—even if just for the inspiration.

Chapter Eleven

Day Trips and Excursions

Český Krumlov: A Fairytale Town

A short journey south of Prague will transport you to Český Krumlov, a town so picturesque it feels like stepping into a storybook. Known for its charming cobblestone streets, pastel-colored houses, and the iconic Český Krumlov Castle, this UNESCO World Heritage Site is one of the most enchanting destinations in the Czech Republic.

What Makes Český Krumlov Special

Nestled along the bends of the Vltava River, Český Krumlov is celebrated for its well-preserved medieval architecture. Walking through the town feels like a journey back in time, with each turn revealing historic buildings, quaint courtyards, and artisan shops. The centerpiece of the town is undoubtedly Český Krumlov Castle, which dominates the skyline and offers sweeping views of the town and surrounding countryside.

Inside the castle, you'll find everything from opulent Renaissance interiors to a Baroque theater, one of the best-preserved of its kind in Europe. The castle gardens, with their fountains and neatly trimmed hedges, make for a peaceful escape.

Practical Information

How to Get There: Český Krumlov is about 2.5 hours from Prague by car or bus. Direct buses, like those operated by FlixBus or RegioJet, offer affordable and convenient travel. The town is compact, so once you arrive, you can explore entirely on foot.

Best Time to Visit: The town is magical year-round, but spring and summer bring lush greenery and outdoor events, while winter transforms it into a cozy, snow-dusted retreat. Visit in December for its charming Christmas markets.

What to Do:

- **Castle Tour:** Don't miss the castle tower for panoramic views. Opt for a guided tour to learn the fascinating history of the Rosenberg family who once ruled the area.
- **Egon Schiele Art Centrum:** A haven for art lovers, this gallery is dedicated to the Austrian painter who spent time in the town.
- **Vltava River Rafting:** During summer, locals and tourists alike enjoy leisurely rafting trips along the scenic river.

Insider Tips

1. **Start Early:** Arrive early in the morning to avoid the crowds, especially in peak season.

2. **Dining Recommendations:** For a meal with a view, head to **Papa's Living Restaurant**, which offers riverside seating and hearty Czech fare.
3. **Hidden Corners:** Venture off the main streets to discover quiet alleys and smaller squares. These spots are perfect for photos and a more peaceful experience.
4. **Stay Overnight:** While Český Krumlov can be done as a day trip, spending the night allows you to experience the magical atmosphere after the day-trippers leave.

Kutná Hora and the Bone Church

If there is one day trip from Prague that combines history, eerie beauty, and architectural brilliance, it's a visit to Kutná Hora. Located about 80 kilometers (50 miles) east of Prague, this medieval town was once a wealthy silver mining center that rivaled Prague in importance during the 14th and 15th centuries. Today, it is a UNESCO World Heritage Site known for its stunning Gothic structures, rich past, and most famously, the hauntingly beautiful Sedlec Ossuary—better known as the Bone Church.

The History and Significance of Kutná Hora

Kutná Hora flourished during the Middle Ages thanks to its vast silver deposits. By the late 13th century, the town had become the economic backbone of the Kingdom of Bohemia, minting coins that circulated across Europe. With wealth came grand architecture, and Kutná Hora soon developed an impressive skyline of Gothic, Baroque, and Renaissance structures. Despite its decline after the mines were exhausted, its historical charm remains intact, drawing visitors from around the world.

The Sedlec Ossuary: The Bone Church

One of the most intriguing and eerie attractions in the Czech Republic, the Sedlec Ossuary is a small chapel decorated with the bones of an estimated 40,000 to 70,000 people. This macabre yet fascinating site dates back to the 13th century when an abbot sprinkled soil from Jerusalem's Golgotha cemetery on the monastery graveyard, making it a sought-after burial site. By the 16th century, the space was overcrowded, and the remains were arranged into artistic formations, culminating in the extraordinary skeletal decor seen today.

The interior of the Bone Church is a chilling yet mesmerizing sight. Chandeliers, coats of arms, and garlands made entirely of human bones adorn the space, serving as a striking reminder of mortality. Despite its unsettling appearance, the ossuary is not meant to be morbid; rather, it symbolizes the Christian belief in resurrection and the transient nature of life.

Other Highlights in Kutná Hora

- **St. Barbara's Cathedral** – A masterpiece of late Gothic architecture, this cathedral is dedicated to the patron saint of miners. Its intricate frescoes depicting medieval life, stunning vaulted ceilings, and breathtaking views from the terrace make it a must-see.

- **The Italian Court (Vlachovský dvůr)** – Once the royal mint of Bohemia, this historical palace showcases the town's silver mining past. Visitors can explore old minting machines, medieval coins, and grand ceremonial halls.
- **The Church of the Assumption of Our Lady and Saint John the Baptist** – Another UNESCO-listed gem, this Baroque-Gothic church features stunning frescoes and an impressive nave.

Practical Information for Visiting Kutná Hora

- **Getting There**: The easiest way to reach Kutná Hora from Prague is by train. Trains from Prague's main station (Hlavní nádraží) take about an hour and run frequently. Once in Kutná Hora, local buses or a 15-minute walk will take you to the Bone Church and other major sites.

- **Admission Fees**: Entrance fees vary, but a combination ticket for multiple sites, including the Sedlec Ossuary and St. Barbara's Cathedral, offers the best value.
- **Best Time to Visit**: Spring and autumn are ideal for avoiding crowds while still enjoying pleasant weather. If visiting in winter, be prepared for shorter daylight hours and chilly temperatures.
- **Insider Tip**: To fully appreciate the eerie atmosphere of the Bone Church, visit early in the morning or late in the afternoon when the crowds are thinner. If you're a photography enthusiast, the dim lighting and dramatic contrasts make for some unforgettable shots.

Karlovy Vary: Spa Heaven

If you're looking for a day trip that combines luxury, history, and natural beauty, Karlovy Vary is the perfect escape from Prague. Known as the most famous spa town in the Czech Republic, this picturesque destination has been attracting visitors for centuries with its mineral-rich hot springs, grand colonnades, and elegant architecture. Whether you're coming for relaxation, sightseeing, or a taste of its famous herbal liqueur, Karlovy Vary offers a unique experience unlike anywhere else in the country.

The Healing Waters of Karlovy Vary

Karlovy Vary, also known as Carlsbad, has been a spa retreat since the 14th century, when Emperor Charles IV reportedly discovered the hot springs' healing properties. Today, the town boasts **13 main thermal springs** and **over 300 smaller ones**, each with varying temperatures and mineral compositions. Visitors can drink the warm, mineral-rich water from the iconic porcelain spa cups available at numerous fountains around the town. Many believe these waters aid digestion, improve metabolism, and promote overall health.

The Stunning Colonnades

One of the highlights of Karlovy Vary is its **ornate colonnades**, which serve as both architectural wonders and public gathering spots for visitors to sample the thermal waters. The most famous include:

- **Mill Colonnade** – The largest and most elegant, featuring 124 Corinthian columns and five mineral springs.
- **Market Colonnade** – A beautiful wooden structure built in Swiss style, sheltering the Charles IV Spring.
- **Park Colonnade** – A charming cast-iron structure surrounded by lush greenery, perfect for a peaceful stroll.

- **Hot Spring Colonnade** – Home to the famous **Vřídlo geyser**, which shoots mineral water up to 12 meters high.

Walking through these colonnades while sipping from a spa cup is a quintessential Karlovy Vary experience.

Indulge in a Spa Treatment

While drinking the thermal waters is a must, Karlovy Vary's real charm lies in its luxurious spa treatments. Many of the town's **historic spa hotels** offer therapies such as **thermal baths, mud wraps, massages, and hydrotherapy**, all designed to rejuvenate the body and mind. Some of the best-known spa resorts include **Hotel Imperial, Grandhotel Pupp, and Elizabeth Baths**. Even if you're visiting just for the day, many spas offer short treatments so you can still enjoy the experience.

Beyond the Spas: Things to See and Do

Karlovy Vary isn't just about relaxation—it's also a visually stunning town with plenty of cultural attractions.

- **Diana Lookout Tower** – For the best panoramic views of Karlovy Vary, take the funicular up to this tower and enjoy breathtaking scenery.

- **Moser Glass Museum** – Discover the town's world-famous **Moser crystal**, known as the "glass of kings." The museum showcases exquisite hand-blown glasswork.
- **Church of St. Mary Magdalene** – A striking Baroque church located near the Hot Spring Colonnade. Its underground crypt holds ancient burial remains.
- **Becherovka Museum** – Learn about Karlovy Vary's signature herbal liqueur, **Becherovka**, and even sample a taste of this Czech specialty.

Practical Information for Your Visit

- **Getting There:** Karlovy Vary is about **2 hours from Prague** by bus or car. Buses run frequently from Florenc Bus Station and are the most convenient option. Trains are available but take longer.
- **Best Time to Visit:** Spring and summer offer the most pleasant weather, but visiting in autumn brings fewer crowds and stunning foliage. The **Karlovy Vary International Film Festival** in July is a major cultural event, drawing movie lovers from around the world.
- **Insider Tip:** While many visitors focus on the spa treatments, don't skip Karlovy Vary's **local wafers**—thin, crispy spa wafers filled with

248

chocolate, hazelnut, or vanilla. They make a delicious snack or souvenir.

Whether you come for the healing waters, luxurious spa treatments, or simply to enjoy the town's breathtaking scenery, Karlovy Vary is a day trip that will leave you feeling refreshed and inspired.

Chapter Twelve

Practical Information for Travelers

Currency, Costs, and Tipping in Prague

Understanding the local currency, typical expenses, and tipping etiquette in Prague can help you navigate the city with confidence. While Prague remains one of the more affordable European capitals, prices can vary depending on where you go. Here's a breakdown of what to expect when handling money in the Czech Republic.

Currency and Payment Methods

The official currency of the Czech Republic is the **Czech koruna (CZK)**, often abbreviated as **Kč**. While some businesses in tourist areas accept euros, they often offer unfavorable exchange rates, so it's best to pay in koruna whenever possible.

- **Exchange Rates:** The exchange rate fluctuates, so check before your trip. As a rough guide, **1 EUR is approximately 25-26 CZK**, and **1 USD is around 22-23 CZK** (but always verify the latest rates).
- **Best Places to Exchange Money:** Avoid airport and hotel exchange offices, as they often charge high fees. Instead, use reputable exchange offices in the city, such as **eXchange** or **Alfa Prague**, which offer fair rates with no hidden fees.
- **ATMs:** The safest way to withdraw koruna is from **bank ATMs** (Česká spořitelna, Komerční banka, Raiffeisenbank). Avoid ATMs labeled "Euronet" or those found in highly touristy areas, as they often charge high withdrawal fees.

- **Cards vs. Cash:** Credit and debit cards are widely accepted in restaurants, shops, and even public transport ticket machines. However, some smaller establishments, market stalls, and local pubs still prefer cash. It's good to have **small denominations** on hand for tipping, public restrooms, or smaller purchases.

Typical Costs in Prague

Prague offers a mix of budget-friendly and upscale experiences. Here's a general idea of what you can expect to spend:

- **Public Transport Ticket:** 30 CZK (90-minute pass)
- **Coffee in a Café:** 60-80 CZK
- **Beer in a Pub:** 50-70 CZK
- **Casual Meal (local restaurant):** 200-350 CZK
- **Mid-range Dinner for Two:** 800-1,200 CZK
- **Museum Entry:** 150-300 CZK
- **Hotel Room (mid-range):** 2,000-4,000 CZK per night

While Prague remains cheaper than cities like Paris or London, prices have been rising, especially in tourist-heavy areas. Dining in **local neighborhoods outside the city center** can save you money.

Tipping Etiquette in Prague

Tipping in Prague is appreciated but not always expected, and customs differ slightly from other European destinations. Here's what you need to know:

- **Restaurants:** A tip of **5-10%** is common for good service. In tourist areas, some places may round up your bill and expect a tip, but this is not mandatory. Unlike in the U.S., tipping is not always included in the bill, so check before leaving extra.
- **Bars & Cafés:** Rounding up to the nearest **10 or 20 CZK** is standard when paying in cash. If you're paying by card, some machines allow you to add a tip before confirming payment.
- **Taxis & Ride-Sharing:** If using a **taxi or Uber**, rounding up the fare or adding 10% is appreciated but not obligatory.
- **Hotels:** If you receive exceptional service from porters or housekeeping, a small tip of **50-100 CZK** is a nice gesture.
- **Tour Guides:** If you enjoyed a walking tour, tipping **50-150 CZK** per person is a good rule of thumb. Some free tours operate on a tip-only basis, so be prepared to give more in those cases.

Money-Saving Tips

- **Use Contactless Payments:** Many places prefer card payments, and this saves you from carrying too much cash.
- **Avoid Tourist Traps:** Restaurants around Old Town Square tend to have inflated prices. Walk a few streets away for more local-friendly rates.
- **Take Advantage of Lunch Deals:** Many restaurants offer **affordable lunch menus (120-200 CZK)**, especially on weekdays.
- **Buy Public Transport Passes:** If using trams or metros frequently, a **24-hour (120 CZK) or 72-hour (330 CZK) pass** is much cheaper than buying single tickets.

Health and Safety Tips

Prague is generally a very safe and traveler-friendly city, but like any major tourist destination, it's important to be mindful of your health and safety. Whether you're strolling through the historic streets, using public transport, or enjoying Prague's famous nightlife, a little preparation can go a long way in ensuring a smooth and hassle-free trip.

Health Tips for Travelers

Medical Services and Pharmacies

- The **Czech Republic has excellent healthcare services**, and Prague has many hospitals and clinics that cater to international visitors.
- **Pharmacies (Lékárna)** are easy to find throughout the city and are your first stop for minor illnesses, over-the-counter medicine, and prescription refills. Most pharmacies are open from **8:00 AM to 6:00 PM**, but **nonstop pharmacies** (such as Lékárna Palackého) are available for emergencies.
- If you need to see a doctor, private clinics like **Canadian Medical, Prague Medical Center, or Unicare Medical** provide services in English.
- In case of **serious medical emergencies**, dial **112** for immediate assistance.

Travel Health Insurance

- **Health insurance is mandatory** for travelers visiting the Czech Republic, especially for those from non-EU countries. While EU citizens can use their **European Health Insurance Card (EHIC)**, it's still recommended to have additional travel insurance.
- A good travel insurance plan should cover **medical emergencies, doctor visits,**

hospital stays, and even trip cancellations.

- If you need **urgent medical care**, be aware that non-EU travelers may need to pay upfront for medical services and then claim reimbursement through their insurance provider.

Staying Healthy While Traveling

- **Tap water is safe to drink** in Prague, so there's no need to buy bottled water. You can refill your water bottle at restaurants, hotels, or public fountains.
- **Local food is generally safe**, but if you have a sensitive stomach, be mindful of rich Czech cuisine, which is heavy on meats and sauces.
- Prague can experience **high air pollution in winter** due to heating emissions, so if you have respiratory conditions, be cautious on days with poor air quality.
- If you're visiting in **summer**, stay hydrated and wear sunscreen, as Prague's cobblestone streets can get **hot and reflective** in direct sunlight.

Safety Tips for a Hassle-Free Trip

Prague is one of the **safest cities in Europe**, but as with any popular destination, it's important to be aware of potential risks.

Pickpocketing and Scams

- Pickpocketing is the **most common crime** in Prague, particularly in crowded areas like **Old Town Square, Charles Bridge, and Wenceslas Square**.
- Be cautious in **public transport**, especially on the **metro and trams 9, 17, and 22**, which are frequently targeted by pickpockets.
- **Keep your valuables secure**: Use a crossbody bag with a zipper, keep wallets in front pockets, and avoid flashing expensive items.
- Watch out for **common scams**, including:
    - **Fake petitions**: Someone may ask you to sign a petition and then demand a donation.
    - **Overcharging taxis**: Always use reputable taxi apps like **Liftago or Uber** instead of hailing a taxi on the street.
    - **Fake money exchange offices**: Some places offer "zero commission" but have terrible exchange rates. Use trusted exchange points.

Street and Traffic Safety

- Prague's historic streets are mostly **cobblestone**, so wear comfortable shoes to avoid slipping or twisting an ankle.
- Always **use designated pedestrian crossings** and be mindful of **trams**, which have the right of way and don't stop quickly.
- **E-scooters and bikes** have become popular, but riding them through pedestrian areas like Old Town Square can result in fines.

Nighttime Safety

- The city is generally safe at night, but stick to well-lit areas and **avoid isolated parks or dark alleyways** late at night.
- If enjoying Prague's nightlife, **drink responsibly** and be mindful of your belongings in crowded bars and clubs.
- Be cautious of **overly friendly strangers** in nightlife areas—sometimes, they work in groups to distract tourists while someone else steals valuables.
- If taking a taxi at night, **use an official app** like Bolt or Uber to avoid being overcharged.

Emergency Contacts in Prague

Knowing emergency numbers and key contacts can be invaluable if you run into any trouble.

- **General Emergency Number (Police, Fire, Ambulance): 112** (works from any phone, no SIM card required)
- **Ambulance: 155**
- **Police: 158**
- **Fire Brigade: 150**
- **Nonstop Pharmacy: +420 224 946 982** (Lékárna Palackého)
- **Tourist Police Hotline: +420 974 841 750** (English-speaking officers available)

Final Safety and Health Tips

- **Keep digital and paper copies** of your passport, insurance, and emergency contacts.
- Be aware of **fake police officers** asking for ID—real officers won't demand on-the-spot fines.
- Trust your instincts—if something feels off, move away from the situation.

Emergency Contacts and Numbers

When traveling, it's always wise to have a list of emergency contacts at hand. While Prague is a relatively safe and well-organized city, unexpected situations can arise, from medical emergencies to lost belongings or transportation issues. Knowing whom to call and where to go can make a huge difference in resolving any problem quickly and efficiently.

General Emergency Numbers

The Czech Republic has a well-functioning emergency response system. The following numbers can be dialed from any phone, including mobiles without a SIM card. Operators typically speak **Czech and English**, though responses may be quicker in Czech.

- **European Emergency Number (General Assistance): 112**
  - Works across the EU and connects you to police, ambulance, or fire services as needed.
  - Recommended for travelers as English-speaking operators are available.
- **Ambulance (Medical Emergencies): 155**
  - Call if you need immediate **medical attention or an ambulance**.
  - Operators may ask for details like location, condition of the patient, and the nearest landmark.

- **Police (Law Enforcement & Crime Reports): 158**
  - If you're a victim of a crime, theft, or need police assistance, call this number.
- **Fire Department: 150**
  - In case of **fire, gas leaks, or other hazardous situations** requiring fire department assistance.

Tourist-Specific Emergency Contacts

- **Tourist Police Hotline (Prague Police Department): +420 974 841 750**
  - Dedicated to helping tourists who have been victims of petty crime, scams, or need police assistance.
  - Officers speaking **English, German, Spanish, and French** are available.
- **Lost & Found Office (City of Prague): +420 222 113 119**
  - If you lose personal belongings in the city (documents, wallets, phones), they might end up in the **Lost & Found Office at Karoliny Světlé 5, Prague 1**.
  - Open weekdays from **8:00 AM to 6:00 PM**.
- **Prague Transport Authority (DPP) Lost & Found: +420 296 191 817**

- If you leave something on a tram, bus, or metro, report it here.
- Located at **Na Bojišti 5, Prague 2**, open weekdays from **7:00 AM to 7:00 PM**.
- **Foreigners' Police: +420 974 841 356**
  - If you need to report **a lost passport or visa issues**, you may be required to visit the Foreigners' Police office.

Medical and Health Emergencies

If you need urgent medical care in Prague, you can go to one of the city's main hospitals with **emergency departments (Pohotovost)**. These hospitals are well-equipped and offer **English-speaking medical staff**.

24/7 Emergency Hospitals in Prague

- **Motol University Hospital (Nemocnice Motol) – Best for Foreigners**
  - **Address:** V Úvalu 84, Prague 5
  - **Phone:** +420 224 431 111
  - **Why go here?** One of the best hospitals for tourists, with English-speaking doctors in most departments.
- **General University Hospital (Všeobecná fakultní nemocnice – VFN)**

- **Address:** U Nemocnice 2, Prague 2
- **Phone:** +420 224 961 111
- **Why go here?** Central location and good for urgent care.
- **Na Homolce Hospital (Nemocnice Na Homolce)**
  - **Address:** Roentgenova 2, Prague 5
  - **Phone:** +420 257 272 350
  - **Why go here?** Private hospital known for high-quality care, often used by expats.

24-Hour Pharmacies (Lékárna)

Pharmacies in Prague are called **lékárna**, and most are open during regular business hours. If you need medication outside of these hours, the following **24/7 pharmacies** are available:

- **Lékárna Palackého – Nonstop pharmacy**
  - **Address:** Palackého 5, Prague 1
  - **Phone:** +420 224 946 982
- **Lékárna BENU at Kotva Shopping Center**
  - **Address:** Revoluční 655/1, Prague 1
  - **Phone:** +420 222 318 282

Embassy and Consulate Contacts

If you lose your passport, need legal assistance, or require consular services, you should contact your country's embassy or consulate in Prague. Below are a few key embassies for common travelers to Prague:

- **United States Embassy**
  - **Address:** Tržiště 15, Prague 1
  - **Phone:** +420 257 022 000
- **United Kingdom Embassy**
  - **Address:** Thunovská 14, Prague 1
  - **Phone:** +420 257 402 111
- **Canadian Embassy**
  - **Address:** Ve Struhách 95/2, Prague 6
  - **Phone:** +420 272 101 800
- **Australian Embassy**
  - **Address:** Muchova 6, Prague 6
  - **Phone:** +420 257 099 400
- **German Embassy**
  - **Address:** Vlašská 19, Prague 1
  - **Phone:** +420 257 113 111

You can find a full list of embassies and consulates on the Czech Ministry of Foreign Affairs website.

Final Tips for Emergencies in Prague

1. **Save important numbers** in your phone before your trip, including your country's embassy, emergency services, and your travel insurance provider.

2. **Always carry a copy of your passport** and visa, especially when going out at night.
3. If you lose your passport, **report it to the Foreigners' Police first**, then contact your embassy.
4. **Use mobile apps like Google Maps, Uber, or Liftago** to navigate and call taxis safely.
5. **Trust official sources**—if you need help, approach hotel staff, police officers, or designated information centers rather than random strangers.

By keeping these contacts and tips in mind, you'll be well-prepared for any situation, ensuring a **stress-free and safe visit to Prague**.

Accessibility and Inclusivity

Prague is a city filled with historic charm, but its medieval streets, cobblestone pathways, and centuries-old architecture can present challenges for travelers with mobility issues. However, the city has made notable progress in improving **accessibility and inclusivity**, particularly in public transportation, accommodations, and cultural sites.

Whether you have mobility limitations, visual impairments, or other accessibility needs, this guide will help you navigate Prague comfortably.

Getting Around Prague with Accessibility in Mind

Prague's public transportation system has been making strides toward becoming more **wheelchair-friendly and accessible**. Here's what you need to know:

Metro (Subway) Accessibility

- The **Prague Metro** is one of the best options for travelers with mobility challenges.
- **Line C (red line)** is the most accessible, with **elevators and step-free access** at nearly all stations.
- **Line A (green line) and Line B (yellow line)** are partially accessible, but some stations still lack **elevators or ramps**.
- A **wheelchair-accessible metro map** is available at **www.dpp.cz** (Prague's transport authority website).

Trams and Buses

- Many **modern low-floor trams (lines 3, 9, 17, and 22)** are wheelchair-friendly, but some older trams still have steps.
- Buses are mostly accessible and often have **ramps for easy entry**.
- If you need **assistance**, Prague's public transport offers a **specialized transport service (Doprava Bez Bariér)**, which can be booked in advance for easier navigation.

Taxis and Rideshares

- **Liftago and Uber** both provide options for passengers with mobility impairments.
- Special **wheelchair-accessible taxis** can be booked through companies like **AA Taxi (+420 222 333 222)** or **Modrý Anděl (+420 737 222 333)**.

Accessible Attractions and Landmarks

While some historic sites in Prague may be **challenging to access due to cobblestones or stairs**, many major attractions have taken steps to become more inclusive:

Fully Accessible Attractions

- **Prague Castle** – The castle complex is partially wheelchair-accessible, with ramps and

elevators available in some areas. The entrance from U Prašného mostu is the best for wheelchair users.

- **Old Town Square** – The square itself is accessible, but the **Astronomical Clock Tower has limited access**.
- **Petřín Hill & Lookout Tower** – A **funicular with wheelchair access** runs up the hill, and the base of the tower is accessible (though the spiral staircase to the top is not).
- **Jewish Quarter** – The Jewish Museum and **Spanish Synagogue** are wheelchair-friendly, but some cemeteries and older buildings have limited access.

Partially Accessible Attractions

- **Charles Bridge** – While the bridge is technically step-free, the **uneven cobblestone surface** can make it difficult for wheelchairs.
- **St. Vitus Cathedral** – The main entrance has **stairs**, but visitors can request access through an alternative **side entrance with a ramp**.
- **National Theatre & Estates Theatre** – Both have **wheelchair-accessible seating**, but it's recommended to call in advance.

Accessible Accommodations in Prague

Many hotels in Prague now offer **barrier-free rooms with step-free access, wide doors, and adapted bathrooms**. Here are some hotels known for their **excellent accessibility**:

- **Motel One Prague** – A **modern hotel with step-free access**, located near Florenc metro station.
- **Hotel Grandior** – Offers **wheelchair-friendly rooms and elevators** with a central location.
- **Hilton Prague** – Fully accessible with **adapted rooms, ramps, and an elevator**.
- **Clarion Congress Hotel Prague** – Features **barrier-free rooms** and is connected to an accessible metro station.

When booking, **contact the hotel in advance** to confirm specific accessibility features.

For Travelers with Visual or Hearing Impairments

Prague is becoming more inclusive for **visually and hearing-impaired travelers**. Here's what you can expect:

- **Tactile paving and audio signals** at major pedestrian crossings help visually impaired travelers navigate safely.

- **Some museums and attractions offer audio guides or sign language tours**, including the National Museum and DOX Centre for Contemporary Art.
- **Mobile apps like Be My Eyes** can connect visually impaired visitors with local volunteers for assistance.

LGBTQ+ Inclusivity in Prague

Prague is one of the most **LGBTQ+-friendly** cities in Central Europe. The city boasts **inclusive nightlife, events, and safe public spaces** for LGBTQ+ travelers.

- **Pride Events:** Prague hosts an annual **Prague Pride Festival** in August, featuring parades, concerts, and cultural discussions.
- **LGBTQ+-Friendly Bars & Clubs:** Q Café, Café Bar Flirt, and Friends Club are popular spots.
- **Inclusive Hotels:** Many international hotel chains, like Marriott and Hilton, openly support LGBTQ+ guests.

Prague is a generally **safe city for LGBTQ+ travelers**, but as with anywhere, it's always good to be aware of your surroundings.

Tips for an Inclusive and Accessible Visit to Prague

✔ **Check accessibility in advance** – Use **www.accessibleprague.com** to check detailed information about hotels, restaurants, and attractions.

✔ **Use Google Maps Street View** – If you're worried about cobblestones or steep paths, check the area virtually before visiting.

✔ **Plan routes using accessible transport** – Low-floor trams and metro stations with **elevators** will make travel easier.

✔ **Book assistance at Prague Airport** – If you need mobility assistance, request it at **least 48 hours before your flight**.

✔ **Download the VoiceMap app** – Some self-guided tours offer **audio descriptions** for visually impaired travelers.

Final Thoughts on Accessibility in Prague

While Prague is still working to become **100% barrier-free**, it has made significant improvements in **transportation, accommodations, and tourist sites**. With careful planning and the right resources, travelers with disabilities or special needs can enjoy a **comfortable, inclusive, and memorable experience** in this stunning city.

Would you like me to include **specific wheelchair routes or resources** for accessible travel?

Chapter Thirteen

Seasonal Events and Festivals

prague Spring International Music Festival

Prague is a city where history and culture intertwine beautifully, and there's no better example of this than the **Prague Spring International Music Festival (Pražské jaro)**. Held annually from **May 12 to**

early June, this world-renowned classical music festival transforms the city into a **melodic paradise**, drawing **top-tier orchestras, conductors, and soloists** from around the globe.

For music lovers, this is the **ultimate cultural event in Prague**, offering an extraordinary opportunity to witness **symphonies, operas, chamber music, and contemporary compositions** performed in some of the city's most breathtaking venues.

History and Legacy of Prague Spring Festival

Founded in **1946**, the festival was initially created to mark the first anniversary of the end of **World War II**. Over the decades, it has grown into one of

Europe's most prestigious classical music festivals, attracting leading musicians such as Leonard Bernstein, Yehudi Menuhin, and Mstislav Rostropovich.

One of its most cherished traditions is the **opening concert on May 12**, which commemorates the anniversary of the death of Czech composer **Bedřich Smetana**. His famous symphonic cycle, *Má vlast (My Homeland)*, is performed annually, setting a powerful and emotional tone for the festival.

Festival Highlights and What to Expect

The Prague Spring Festival spans several weeks, offering a **diverse program of performances** that appeal to both classical purists and contemporary music fans. Here's what you can expect:

✔ **World-Class Orchestras & Soloists** – Expect performances by legendary ensembles like the **Czech Philharmonic Orchestra, Vienna Philharmonic, and London Symphony Orchestra**.

✔ **Prestigious Venues** – Concerts take place in stunning settings such as **Rudolfinum's Dvořák Hall, the Municipal House's Smetana Hall, and the Estates Theatre**, immersing audiences in both **musical brilliance and architectural beauty**.

✔ **Contemporary and Experimental Music** – While classical music is the heart of the festival, there are also performances of **modern compositions, jazz concerts, and experimental collaborations**, ensuring there's something for every music enthusiast.

✔ **Masterclasses and Workshops** – Beyond concerts, the festival hosts **educational programs, lectures, and public masterclasses** where visitors can gain insights into the world of classical music.

✔ **International Talent Competition** – The **Prague Spring International Music Competition**, held as part of the festival, showcases rising stars in classical music and has launched the careers of many celebrated musicians.

Venues: Where to Experience Prague Spring Festival

The festival's concerts take place in **some of Prague's most exquisite historical venues**, each adding its own charm to the performances:

- **Rudolfinum (Dvořák Hall)** – The festival's main venue, offering **excellent acoustics** and an intimate atmosphere.

- **Municipal House (Smetana Hall)** – A beautifully **ornate Art Nouveau concert hall**, home to major symphonic performances.
- **Estates Theatre** – Famous for hosting Mozart's *Don Giovanni* premiere, this venue is ideal for opera and chamber music.
- **St. Agnes Convent** – A hidden gem for **chamber music lovers**, offering a peaceful and intimate setting.
- **Church of St. Simon and St. Jude** – Known for **baroque and organ concerts**, this church adds a spiritual dimension to the festival.

Practical Information for Visitors

If you're planning to attend **Prague Spring International Music Festival**, here are a few **insider tips** to make your experience smoother:

✔ **Book Tickets in Advance** – Concerts sell out quickly, so it's best to book your tickets online at **www.festival.cz** as soon as sales open (typically in early winter).

✔ **Dress Code** – While Prague is a relaxed city, **classical music events are elegant affairs**. Dressing in **smart casual or semi-formal attire** is recommended, especially for evening performances.

✔ **Arrive Early** – Many venues have **assigned seating**, but arriving early ensures you have time to soak in the ambiance and enjoy the pre-concert atmosphere.

✔ **Explore Festival Packages** – Some travel agencies and hotels offer **festival packages** that include concert tickets, guided city tours, and accommodations.

✔ **Combine Music with Sightseeing** – The festival's venues are **close to major landmarks**, so you can easily explore **Old Town, Prague Castle, or Charles Bridge** before or after a performance.

Why You Shouldn't Miss the Prague Spring Festival

Even if you're not a classical music enthusiast, the **Prague Spring Festival is an experience like no other**. It's more than just a series of concerts—it's a celebration of art, history, and Prague's rich musical heritage. Attending a performance in one of the city's **grand concert halls or historic churches** is a magical way to experience the **soul of Prague**.

For those who love **music, culture, and unforgettable travel moments**, Prague in spring is simply **unmissable**.

Christmas Markets and Winter Festivities

When winter blankets Prague in a dusting of snow, the city transforms into a **magical wonderland**, glowing with festive lights, the scent of mulled wine in the air, and the warmth of traditional holiday traditions. Prague's Christmas markets are among the most **enchanting in Europe**, offering visitors a perfect blend of history, culture, and seasonal cheer. Running from late November until early January, these markets bring the city's most picturesque squares to life, creating an unforgettable holiday atmosphere

The Best Christmas Markets in Prague

Prague's Christmas markets are scattered across the city, but a few stand out as must-visit destinations.

Old Town Square Christmas Market
The heart of Prague's festive celebrations beats in Old Town Square, where the city's largest and most famous Christmas market is held. A towering, beautifully decorated Christmas tree stands at the center, illuminated nightly in a mesmerizing display. Wooden stalls surround the square, selling

handcrafted ornaments, winter accessories, and delicious Czech holiday treats. Carol singers and live performances add to the atmosphere, making it an essential stop for any visitor.

Wenceslas Square Christmas Market
Just a short walk from Old Town Square, Wenceslas Square hosts another vibrant market, slightly less crowded but equally festive. It's a great place to shop for traditional gifts like wooden toys, glassware, and embroidered textiles. The market's food stands offer some of the best local winter delicacies, from sausages to freshly baked pastries.

Prague Castle Christmas Market
Set against the breathtaking backdrop of Prague Castle, this market has a **fairy-tale-like** ambiance, with smaller crowds and a more intimate feel. The historic setting adds charm, and the selection of **locally made handicrafts, gingerbread cookies, and Czech ceramics** makes it an excellent place for unique souvenirs.

Náměstí Míru Christmas Market
A favorite among locals, this market is held in front of the stunning **Church of St. Ludmila**. It's a quieter alternative to the city center markets and offers a more **authentic, community-oriented experience**. Here, you'll find high-quality handmade gifts and a welcoming atmosphere.

Traditional Czech Christmas Treats

No visit to Prague's Christmas markets is complete without indulging in some **classic Czech holiday treats**. Vendors offer a tempting selection of seasonal delicacies, each with its own unique flavors and traditions.

- **Trdelník** – A popular sweet pastry, rolled in cinnamon sugar and sometimes filled with chocolate or ice cream. While not traditionally Czech, it has become a beloved holiday snack.
- **Svařák (Mulled Wine)** – A warm, spiced red wine that is perfect for keeping the cold at bay while wandering through the festive streets.
- **Perníčky (Gingerbread Cookies)** – Beautifully decorated and often sold in charming shapes, these cookies are a staple of Czech Christmas celebrations.
- **Vánočka** – A braided Christmas bread similar to brioche, traditionally eaten on Christmas morning.
- **Roasted Chestnuts and Almonds** – A seasonal favorite, adding to the cozy and nostalgic feel of the markets.

Winter Festivities and Traditions

Beyond the markets, Prague offers a variety of **festive events and traditions** that make the holiday season truly special.

Christmas Eve Traditions
In the Czech Republic, **December 24th is the most important day of Christmas celebrations**. Families gather for a festive dinner, which traditionally features **fried carp and potato salad**. According to local folklore, those who fast during the day may see a golden pig, symbolizing good luck.

Midnight Mass at St. Vitus Cathedral
For a more spiritual experience, many visitors and locals attend the **midnight mass at St. Vitus Cathedral** on Christmas Eve. The grand Gothic

interior, lit by candlelight, creates an unforgettable atmosphere of peace and reverence.

New Year's Eve in Prague

As the Christmas markets wind down, Prague prepares for its spectacular **New Year's Eve celebrations**. The city is known for its impressive fireworks display over the **Vltava River**, best viewed from **Charles Bridge, Letná Park, or the Petrin Hill viewpoint**. Restaurants and bars host special dinners and parties, making it a lively night to ring in the new year.

Practical Information for Visitors

- **Best Time to Visit** – The Christmas markets typically open in **late November and run until early January**, with the best time to visit being **early December** when the festive decorations are at their peak but the crowds are still manageable.
- **Weather and Packing Tips** – Prague can be **quite cold in winter**, with temperatures often dropping below freezing. Warm coats, scarves, gloves, and **comfortable winter boots** are essential for enjoying the outdoor markets.
- **Currency and Payments** – While many stalls accept **credit cards**, it's always a good

idea to carry some **Czech koruna (CZK)** for smaller vendors and food stalls.

- **Getting Around** – The markets are well-connected by public transport, and Prague's **trams and metro** make it easy to hop between locations. Walking is also a great way to soak in the festive atmosphere.

Why You Should Experience Christmas in Prague

Prague during the holiday season is a **dream come true** for those who love **Christmas markets, old-world charm, and winter magic**. The twinkling lights, warm drinks, and centuries-old traditions make it an unforgettable experience.

Whether you're shopping for **handmade gifts**, tasting seasonal delicacies, or simply enjoying the festive spirit, Prague's Christmas markets and winter festivities offer a **perfect holiday escape**.

Other Annual Celebrations

Beyond its famous Christmas markets and world-class music festivals, Prague hosts a diverse range of **annual celebrations** that showcase the city's vibrant culture, traditions, and artistic creativity. From centuries-old customs to modern festivals, there's always something happening in Prague that gives visitors a deeper insight into its **rich heritage and dynamic energy**.

Easter Markets and Festivities (March/April)

Just as Prague dazzles during Christmas, its **Easter celebrations** bring another round of colorful markets and joyful traditions. Held primarily in **Old Town Square and Wenceslas Square**, the Easter markets feature **hand-painted eggs (kraslice), traditional Czech crafts, and festive delicacies** like **mazanec (Easter bread) and beránek (lamb-shaped cake).**

A highlight of the Easter season is the **pomlázka tradition**, where young boys gently whip girls with braided willow branches, a folk custom believed to bring health and vitality. Though largely symbolic today, it remains an **authentic Czech Easter experience**.

Witches' Night (Čarodějnice) – The Czech Walpurgis Night (April 30)

One of the most unique and **intriguing Czech traditions** is **Čarodějnice**, or Witches' Night, held on April 30th. This centuries-old pagan festival, similar to Halloween, marks the arrival of **spring** with bonfires, music, and lively celebrations across the country.

In Prague, locals gather in **parks and open spaces**—notably on **Ladronka Park** and **Kampa Island**—to watch **effigies of witches being burned on bonfires**, symbolizing the end of winter and the triumph of light over darkness. The event is **family-friendly**, with **food stalls, live music, and activities for children**, making it a great way for visitors to experience **authentic Czech folklore**.

Prague Fringe Festival (May/June)

For theater lovers, the **Prague Fringe Festival** is a must-see event. Inspired by the **Edinburgh Fringe Festival**, this **independent arts festival** showcases performances from around the world, including **experimental theater, comedy, cabaret, and live music**.

Held in **small venues around Malá Strana**, the festival offers an **intimate and immersive experience**, often featuring **up-and-coming artists** pushing creative boundaries. It's a great opportunity to enjoy **alternative performing arts** while exploring Prague's charming historic district.

United Islands of Prague Festival (June)

Each summer, the banks of the **Vltava River** come alive with music during the **United Islands of Prague Festival**. This **free, multi-genre music festival** transforms Prague's islands—such as **Střelecký Island and Kampa Island**—into vibrant concert venues featuring **local and international artists**.

The festival's focus on **new music trends and emerging talent** makes it a favorite among **young travelers and music enthusiasts**. Whether you enjoy **indie, electronic, rock, or folk**, United Islands of Prague offers an **energetic summer vibe** in one of the city's most scenic settings.

St. Wenceslas Day – Czech Statehood Day (September 28)

Celebrated in honor of **St. Wenceslas, the patron saint of the Czech Republic**, this national holiday is a **time of reflection and cultural pride**. The main festivities take place in **Stará Boleslav**, the town where Wenceslas was martyred in 935 AD, with **pilgrimages, religious ceremonies, and historical reenactments**.

In Prague, visitors can witness **concerts, parades, and special exhibitions** at **Wenceslas Square** and **St. Vitus Cathedral**, where Wenceslas' relics are displayed. It's an excellent time to **learn about Czech history and heritage**, as many **museums and cultural institutions** offer **free or discounted entry** on this day.

Signal Festival – Prague's Festival of Lights (October)

One of the **most visually stunning events in Prague**, the **Signal Festival** transforms the city's historic streets, buildings, and public spaces into a **canvas of light and technology**. For four nights in October, Prague's most famous landmarks—including **Charles Bridge, Old Town Square, and Klementinum**—are illuminated with **dazzling 3D projections, interactive installations, and digital art displays**.

Attracting both locals and tourists, the festival offers an entirely **new perspective of Prague** at night, blending its **Gothic and Baroque architecture with cutting-edge light technology**. Walking through the glowing streets of Prague during the Signal Festival is an **unforgettable experience**.

Velvet Revolution Day – Celebrating Freedom (November 17)

On November 17th, Prague commemorates the **Velvet Revolution**, the peaceful protest movement that led to the end of communist rule in Czechoslovakia in 1989. This historic day is marked by **memorial events, concerts, and public gatherings**, particularly along **Národní třída**, where student demonstrations first took place.

Visitors can **explore exhibitions, attend lectures, and watch documentaries** about the revolution's impact. It's a day filled with **reflection and gratitude**, making it a meaningful time to be in Prague and witness **Czech democracy in action**.

Why You Should Experience Prague's Annual Celebrations

Prague's **year-round calendar of festivals and events** ensures that no matter when you visit, you'll encounter something **culturally enriching, exciting, and uniquely Czech**. Whether you're drawn to the **traditional customs of Easter and Witches' Night**, the **artistic flair of Fringe and Signal Festival**, or the **historical significance of St. Wenceslas and Velvet Revolution Day**, Prague's celebrations **bring the city's spirit to life** in unforgettable ways.

If you want to **see Prague beyond its iconic sights**, experiencing one of its annual festivals is a perfect way to **connect with the local culture, traditions, and community**.

Chapter Fourteen

Sustainable Travel in Prague

Eco-Friendly Accommodations

Prague, with its medieval charm and modern conveniences, is increasingly embracing **sustainable tourism**. As travelers become more conscious of their environmental impact, the city has responded with a growing number of **eco-friendly accommodations** that combine **comfort, sustainability, and authentic experiences**.

From **green-certified hotels** to **boutique stays with eco-conscious practices**, there are plenty of options for visitors looking to minimize their footprint while enjoying Prague's beauty.

Sustainable Hotels: Where to Stay with a Green Conscience

Many hotels in Prague are adopting **eco-friendly initiatives**, such as **energy-efficient lighting, water conservation systems, and waste reduction programs**. Some go even further, incorporating **locally sourced food, fair-trade products, and carbon offset programs** into their business models.

Top Eco-Friendly Hotels in Prague

- **Mosaic House Design & Wellness Hotel**
  A standout example of **sustainable luxury**, Mosaic House was Prague's **first carbon-neutral hotel**. It features **rainwater recycling systems, solar panels, and energy-efficient heating and cooling**. The hotel's design also emphasizes **natural materials** and **minimal waste**, making it a great choice for eco-conscious travelers.
- **Hotel Adria Prague**
  Located near Wenceslas Square, this hotel holds the prestigious **EU Ecolabel certification**, recognizing its commitment to **waste reduction, energy efficiency, and responsible sourcing**. It also partners with local producers for its in-house restaurant, ensuring **fresh, seasonal cuisine**.
- **Miss Sophie's Hotel**
  A charming boutique hotel with a **focus on sustainability**, Miss Sophie's is known for its **repurposed furniture, low-energy lighting, and locally sourced toiletries**. It provides a cozy, **eco-conscious stay in the heart of Prague**.

Eco-Conscious Hostels and Guesthouses

For budget travelers who still want to **support sustainability**, Prague offers a selection of

eco-friendly hostels and guesthouses that prioritize green living.

- **Czech Inn Hostel** – This stylish yet affordable option has **energy-efficient facilities** and a commitment to **recycling and reducing waste**.
- **Sir Toby's Hostel** – A favorite among backpackers, Sir Toby's uses **second-hand furniture**, practices **waste minimization**, and supports **local businesses** in its café and bar.
- **Post Hostel Prague** – This **small, locally owned hostel** focuses on **sustainability and community engagement**, offering **bike rentals and eco-friendly amenities**.

Green Practices to Look for in Accommodations

When booking a place to stay in Prague, look for hotels and guesthouses that follow **eco-friendly practices** such as:

✔ **Renewable Energy Use** – Hotels that utilize **solar panels or energy-efficient heating** contribute to a lower carbon footprint.

✔ **Water Conservation Measures** – Features like **low-flow showers, towel reuse programs, and rainwater harvesting** help conserve water.

✔ **Waste Reduction and Recycling** – Hotels with **plastic-free policies, refillable toiletries, and robust recycling programs** show a commitment to sustainability.

✔ **Locally Sourced and Organic Food** – Restaurants and hotels that use **seasonal, local ingredients** support small producers and reduce food miles.

✔ **Bicycle Rentals and Public Transport Partnerships** – Some accommodations encourage guests to explore Prague sustainably by offering **bikes or public transport passes**.

Why Choosing Eco-Friendly Stays Matters

Opting for an eco-friendly stay isn't just about reducing **your travel footprint**—it also helps support local communities, conserve natural resources, and encourage responsible tourism practices.

By choosing accommodations that prioritize sustainability, travelers can contribute to **Prague's green future** while still enjoying its **stunning architecture, rich history, and vibrant culture**. Sustainable travel doesn't mean sacrificing comfort—it means **making conscious choices that benefit both the environment and the people who call Prague home**.

Supporting Local Businesses

One of the most impactful ways to travel sustainably in Prague is by **supporting local businesses**. Choosing **locally owned shops, restaurants, and experiences** not only enriches your trip with authentic encounters but also helps preserve the city's unique culture and economy. Unlike large international chains, **family-run businesses and independent artisans** reinvest in their communities, ensuring that Prague maintains its charm and traditions for generations to come.

Why Supporting Local Matters

Many of Prague's small businesses face challenges due to mass tourism and globalization. Tourists who choose **local over corporate** make a real difference by:

✔ **Keeping Traditions Alive** – Prague's **handcrafted goods, traditional recipes, and artisanal crafts** have been passed down for centuries. Supporting local businesses ensures these cultural treasures don't disappear.

✔ **Reducing the Environmental Impact** – Local products often have a **smaller carbon footprint** than mass-produced imports, as they don't require extensive shipping.

✔ **Boosting the Economy** – Money spent at local businesses **stays within the community**, helping small entrepreneurs thrive rather than feeding global corporations.

✔ **Providing More Authentic Experiences** – Whether it's a **cozy café, a boutique hotel, or a handmade souvenir**, local businesses offer a personal touch that enhances the travel experience.

Where to Shop Local in Prague

1. Handmade Crafts and Souvenirs
Skip the mass-produced trinkets and look for

authentic Czech-made souvenirs. Prague is famous for:

- **Bohemian Crystal** – Look for shops that sell **locally crafted glassware** instead of imported imitations. Reputable places include **Moser and Artěl**.
- **Wooden Toys and Puppets** – Traditional **hand-carved marionettes** can be found in shops like **Rici Marionettes** or **Truhlář Marionety**.
- **Czech Porcelain** – **Český Porcelán** and **Thun 1794** offer beautiful hand-painted ceramics made in the Czech Republic.
- **Garnet Jewelry** – Authentic **Czech garnet** is a popular souvenir, but be sure to buy from certified retailers like **Granát Turnov**.

2. Locally Owned Cafés and Restaurants

Many of Prague's independent restaurants use **seasonal, locally sourced ingredients**, making them both sustainable and delicious choices. Some great options include:

- **Café Louvre** – A historic café serving **traditional Czech dishes and locally roasted coffee**.
- **Eska** – A modern Czech restaurant using **farm-to-table ingredients** in creative ways.

- **Kantýna** – Specializing in **locally sourced meats and produce**, this eatery supports Czech farmers.
- **Lokál** – A casual restaurant chain that focuses on **fresh, local ingredients and traditional Czech recipes**.

3. Farmers' Markets
For a taste of Prague's **seasonal produce and handmade delicacies**, visit one of the city's vibrant farmers' markets. These markets support **local farmers, bakers, and artisans**, and they're a fantastic way to experience the city like a local.

- **Náplavka Farmers' Market** – Held along the Vltava River, this market is known for its **organic fruits, fresh pastries, and homemade cheeses**.
- **Jiřák Farmers' Market** – Located in Jiřího z Poděbrad Square, this market offers a **wide variety of farm-fresh produce and Czech delicacies**.
- **Dejvice Farmers' Market** – A favorite among locals, this market features **regional specialties, craft beers, and handmade products**.

How to Support Local Businesses Beyond Shopping

✔ **Book Tours with Local Guides** – Instead of large tour operators, choose **small, locally owned tour companies** that offer unique experiences. Walking tours by **Prague City Adventures** or food tours by **Taste of Prague** are great choices.

✔ **Stay in Family-Owned Accommodations** – Many charming guesthouses and boutique hotels in Prague are **locally owned and operated**, offering a more personal and authentic stay.

✔ **Use Local Transportation** – Instead of taxis or ride-sharing apps, take **trams, metro, or rent bikes** from local businesses.

Small Choices, Big Impact

Supporting local businesses isn't just about buying souvenirs—it's about making **mindful choices** that benefit **the community, the environment, and your overall experience**. When you shop, dine, and explore Prague through **locally owned establishments**, you become part of the city's story in a meaningful way. Your contribution helps ensure that Prague's rich history, traditions, and small businesses continue to thrive for future travelers to enjoy.

Reducing Your Travel Footprint

Traveling to a city as historic and beautiful as Prague comes with a responsibility to explore **consciously and sustainably**. While tourism fuels the local economy, it can also strain resources, increase pollution, and contribute to overcrowding. The good news? Small, mindful choices can make a big difference. By adjusting how you **move around the city, consume resources, and interact with the local environment**, you can reduce your travel footprint and leave Prague just as stunning as you found it.

1. Opt for Sustainable Transportation

Prague is a **compact, walkable city**, making it easy to explore without relying on carbon-heavy transportation. Instead of taxis or rental cars, consider these greener alternatives:

✔ **Walking** – The best way to take in Prague's charm is on foot. Many top attractions, including Old Town Square, Charles Bridge, and Prague Castle, are within **walking distance of each other**.

✔ **Public Transport** – Prague's **trams, buses, and metro system** are efficient, affordable, and environmentally friendly. The city has been actively working on making public transport more sustainable, with many trams running on **low-emission energy sources**.

✔ **Bike Rentals and E-Scooters** – Services like **Rekola (bike-sharing) and Lime (e-scooters)** allow you to cover more ground without adding to pollution.

Insider Tip: If you're staying in Prague for a few days, get a **Prague Travel Pass**, which provides unlimited access to public transport, saving both money and energy.

2. Choose Low-Waste Dining and Shopping

Many restaurants, markets, and cafés in Prague are adopting **eco-friendly initiatives** by reducing plastic use, sourcing local ingredients, and minimizing waste. You can do your part by:

✔ **Bringing a Reusable Water Bottle** – Prague's tap water is **clean and safe to drink**, so skip the bottled water and refill your own bottle at public fountains or restaurants.

✔ **Avoiding Single-Use Plastics** – Bring a **reusable shopping bag, coffee cup, and cutlery** to reduce plastic waste.

✔ **Dining at Restaurants that Minimize Food Waste** – Many Prague eateries, like **Eska, Spojka Karlín, and MyRaw Café**, focus on **zero-waste cooking and locally sourced ingredients**.

Insider Tip: Visit **Prague's farmers' markets** for fresh, local produce and **plastic-free shopping**. Náplavka and Jiřák markets are fantastic for organic foods, fresh bread, and homemade treats.

3. Stay in Sustainable Accommodations

Where you stay has a direct impact on your travel footprint. Consider **eco-friendly hotels and guesthouses** that take steps to **conserve energy, reduce waste, and support local communities**. Many of Prague's sustainable accommodations offer:

✔ **Energy-efficient lighting and appliances**
✔ **Water conservation systems**
✔ **Locally sourced, organic food options**
✔ **Recycling programs**

Insider Tip: Look for hotels with **Green Key or EU Ecolabel certifications**, such as **Mosaic House or Hotel Adria**, which follow strict sustainability guidelines.

4. Respect the Local Environment and Heritage

Prague's **historic sites, green spaces, and cobblestone streets** have stood the test of time, but they require care to stay intact for future generations. Help protect the city by:

✔ **Avoiding Littering** – Dispose of trash properly and recycle whenever possible.
✔ **Sticking to Marked Paths** – Whether you're in a **historic district or a nature park**, avoid damaging the surroundings by **staying on designated paths**.
✔ **Being Mindful of Noise Pollution** – Prague's neighborhoods, especially Old Town and Malá Strana, are home to locals who appreciate quiet, particularly at night.

5. Travel During Off-Peak Seasons

Prague sees a surge of tourists in **summer (June–August) and during the Christmas season**, which can strain local infrastructure. If your schedule allows, **visit in spring or autumn** when crowds are smaller, and the city's natural beauty is just as breathtaking. Off-season travel helps:

✔ **Reduce over-tourism and its environmental impact**
✔ **Support local businesses during slower periods**

✔ **Provide a more relaxed and authentic experience**

Insider Tip: If you must visit in peak months, explore early in the morning or later in the evening to avoid the crowds while still enjoying Prague's magic.

6. Offset Your Carbon Footprint

If you're flying to Prague, your trip comes with an unavoidable **carbon footprint**. However, you can **balance this impact** by:

✔ **Choosing direct flights** – Take-offs and landings generate the most emissions, so non-stop flights are more eco-friendly.
✔ **Using carbon offset programs** – Many airlines and independent organizations, such as **MyClimate or Gold Standard**, allow travelers to **fund renewable energy projects** to offset emissions.

Every Choice Counts

Reducing your travel footprint isn't about perfection—it's about **small, intentional decisions** that collectively make a big difference. From walking more and supporting sustainable businesses to respecting Prague's historical treasures, each mindful action contributes to a **greener, more responsible** way to explore the world. By making sustainable choices, you'll not only experience Prague in a **more authentic and rewarding way**, but you'll also help preserve its beauty for future travelers.

Chapter Fifteen

Conclusion

Making the Most of Your Prague Adventure

Prague is more than just a city of beautiful architecture and historical landmarks—it's a place that **invites you to slow down, immerse yourself in its culture, and truly experience its magic**. Whether you're here for a few days or an extended stay, the key to making the most of your adventure lies in **balancing sightseeing with** spontaneous discoveries, embracing local traditions, and stepping beyond the usual tourist trails.

1. Balance Must-See Sights with Local Experiences

While iconic landmarks like **Prague Castle, Charles Bridge, and Old Town Square** are essential, your experience will be much richer if you mix these with moments that **connect you to the city on a deeper level**.

✔ **Go beyond the postcard views** – Visit historical neighborhoods like **Vinohrady, Holešovice, and Žižkov**, where you'll find a mix of local culture, art, and unique cafés away from the crowds.

✔ **Experience everyday life** – Instead of just visiting tourist attractions, spend time at **local farmers' markets, cozy bookstores, and independent art galleries** to see Prague through the eyes of its residents.

✔ **Take a break in a quiet spot** – Prague has many **hidden gardens and peaceful courtyards** where you can rest and soak in the moment. Parks like **Vojan Gardens and Havlíčkovy Sady** offer a peaceful retreat from the busy streets.

Insider Tip: Early mornings and late evenings are the best times to visit famous landmarks if you want to experience them without the crowds.

2. Let Food and Drink Be Part of the Adventure

Czech cuisine is more than just **svíčková (marinated beef with creamy sauce) and trdelník (chimney cake)**—it's a cultural experience that tells the story of the country's traditions.

✔ **Try traditional and modern Czech dishes** – Don't just stick to well-known foods; explore dishes like **kulajda (creamy mushroom soup) and smažený sýr (fried cheese)** at both traditional taverns and modern bistros.

✔ **Enjoy Prague's café culture** – Coffee lovers should visit historic cafés like **Café Louvre and Café Slavia**, where writers and intellectuals once gathered.

✔ **Discover the beer culture** – Even if you're not a big beer drinker, visiting a **local brewery or beer garden** is a must. Places like **Letná Beer Garden and Lokál** offer a relaxed setting to enjoy the country's legendary brews.

Insider Tip: If you want to explore Prague's food scene beyond restaurants, consider joining a **food tour** to discover hidden eateries and local markets.

3. Walk, Wander, and Get Lost

One of the best ways to experience Prague is simply by **wandering with no fixed plan**. The city's **cobblestone streets, medieval alleys, and charming squares** hide endless surprises.

✔ **Follow the locals** – If you see a street filled with Prague residents but few tourists, chances are you're about to discover something special.

✔ **Explore by night** – The city takes on a completely different atmosphere after dark. Strolling across **Charles Bridge at midnight or exploring the illuminated courtyards of Prague Castle** can be an unforgettable experience.

✔ **Take a tram ride for the views** – Tram #22 is famous for its scenic route, passing some of the city's most beautiful spots, including the **National Theatre, Prague Castle, and Strahov Monastery**.

Insider Tip: If you love photography, take a walk at sunrise to capture Prague at its quietest and most magical.

4. Respect the City and Its Traditions

While Prague is a popular destination, it's still home to **locals who appreciate visitors who respect**

their culture and daily life. To make the most of your trip while being a responsible traveler:

✔️ **Learn a few Czech phrases** – A simple "Dobrý den" (Good day) or "Děkuji" (Thank you) goes a long way in showing respect to locals.

✔️ **Be mindful of noise in historic areas** – Many locals live in the Old Town, and loud noise at night can be disruptive.

✔️ **Follow local customs** – For example, when **taking public transport, always validate your ticket**, and in restaurants, it's common courtesy to say "dobrou chuť" (enjoy your meal) before eating.

Insider Tip: If you want to avoid tourist traps, check where **locals dine and shop**—these places usually offer **better quality and authentic experiences**.

5. Plan Ahead, But Stay Open to Surprises

A little planning can help make your Prague trip smoother, but **leave room for spontaneity**. Some of the best experiences happen when you allow yourself to explore without a strict schedule.

✔️ **Book tickets in advance for popular attractions** – This helps you **skip long lines** and make the most of your time.

✔️ **Leave space for unexpected discoveries** – Whether it's **a street musician playing in a** hidden courtyard or a pop-up art exhibit in a historic building, some of Prague's most memorable moments aren't in any guidebook.

✔ **Talk to locals** – Prague residents often have the best recommendations, from **where to find the best beer to which streets offer the best sunset views**.

Insider Tip: If your schedule allows, visit Prague on a **weekday** rather than a weekend to avoid the heaviest tourist crowds.

6. Capture the Moment, But Don't Forget to Be Present

It's tempting to **photograph everything**, but don't forget to **pause, look around, and take in Prague with your own eyes**. Some experiences—like the way the sun sets over the **Vltava River** or the sound of a violinist playing on a quiet street—are best enjoyed without a camera in hand.

✔ **Put your phone away sometimes** – You'll remember the moment more vividly if you experience it fully.

✔ **Write down your favorite moments** – Keeping a small travel journal can be a wonderful way to reflect on your journey.

✔ **Share your experience, but live it first** –

Social media can wait; the magic of Prague is happening in real time.

Prague: A City to Be Experienced, Not Just Seen

To truly make the most of your Prague adventure, **immerse yourself in its stories, savor its flavors, and embrace the unexpected**. Whether you're **standing atop Petřín Hill, wandering through a quiet garden, or listening to street musicians in Old Town Square**, Prague is a city that rewards those who take the time to experience it fully.

Let curiosity guide your journey, and **Prague will leave you with unforgettable memories, countless stories, and a longing to return.**

Final Tips and Reflections

As your journey through Prague comes to an end, it's worth taking a moment to reflect on everything you've experienced. This city is more than just its famous sights—it's a place that invites you to **slow down, explore, and connect with its rich culture,**

history, and everyday life. Whether you've walked across Charles Bridge at sunrise, discovered a hidden café in a quiet neighborhood, or watched the golden hues of the Vltava River at sunset, Prague has undoubtedly left an imprint on your heart.

To wrap up your adventure, here are some **final tips and reflections** to help you make the most of your trip, ensure a smooth departure, and leave with memories that will stay with you long after you've gone.

1. Give Yourself Time to Absorb the Experience

It's easy to rush from one attraction to the next, but some of the most meaningful moments happen when you **pause, observe, and simply take in your surroundings**.

✔ **Find a quiet moment before you leave** – Whether it's sitting on a park bench in Letná, taking one last stroll through Old Town Square, or sipping a coffee in a historic café, let yourself **soak in the city one last time**.

✔ **Write down your favorite memories** – A travel journal, a collection of photos, or even just a few notes on your phone will help you relive the magic of Prague whenever you want.

2. Practical Tips for a Smooth Departure

Leaving Prague can be just as important as arriving. A bit of preparation will **make your departure stress-free** and ensure you leave with nothing but good memories.

✔ **Check transportation options in advance** – If you're flying out, give yourself extra time to get to Václav Havel Airport. Public transport is reliable, but traffic can be unpredictable. Consider taking the **Airport Express bus or a pre-booked transfer**.

✔ **Spend any leftover Czech crowns** – Before heading home, use up your Czech currency on **small souvenirs, snacks, or a last-minute beer at the airport**—you might not need crowns in your next destination.

✔ **Confirm your documents** – Double-check that you have your **passport, tickets, and any necessary visas** before heading to the airport or train station.

3. What to Take Home Beyond Souvenirs

Sure, Prague has plenty of beautiful souvenirs—from **handmade crystal to traditional marionettes**—but some of the best things to take home aren't things at all.

✔ **New perspectives** – Prague's mix of history and modernity, old traditions and youthful energy, offers a unique way of looking at the world. Take that sense of curiosity with you.

✔ **A love for slow travel** – This city reminds us that **rushing isn't always the best way to experience a place**. Let your time in Prague inspire you to explore future destinations at a more relaxed pace.

✔ **A desire to return** – Prague is the kind of city that calls you back. Maybe next time, you'll visit in a different season, explore new neighborhoods, or come for one of its world-famous festivals.

4. Staying Connected to Prague After You Leave

Even after your trip ends, there are ways to **keep a little piece of Prague with you** and continue exploring its culture from afar.

✔ **Read Czech literature** – Writers like **Franz Kafka, Milan Kundera, and Bohumil Hrabal** offer deep insights into Prague's soul.

✔ **Listen to Czech music** – Classical legends like **Dvořák and Smetana**, as well as contemporary Czech artists, can transport you back to Prague through sound.

✔ **Try Czech recipes at home** – If you fell in love with **svíčková, goulash, or koláče**, why not try making them yourself? Many Czech dishes can be recreated in your own kitchen.

5. Final Thoughts: A City That Stays with You

Prague is not just a destination—it's a feeling, a story, a moment frozen in time. It's **the soft glow of lanterns along the Vltava, the laughter echoing from a local beer hall, the quiet beauty of a hidden courtyard**. Whether this was your first visit or one of many, **Prague has a way of leaving an imprint on your heart**.

Travel is not just about **seeing places**; it's about the way they **change us**. As you say goodbye to Prague, take a deep breath, smile, and know that this city will always be here, ready to welcome you back.

Safe travels—until next time!

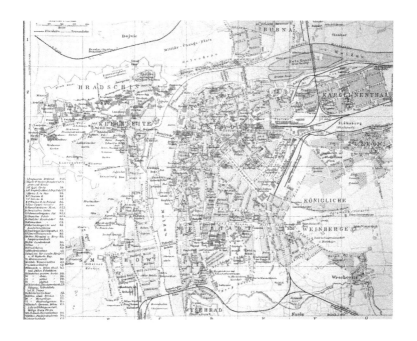

320

Made in the USA
Monee, IL
20 March 2025

14297640R00177